Moving On From Life's Challenges

By Mindy Briggs

Moving On From Life's Challenges

Published by Starnes Books LLC
Edited by Carpenter Editing Services, LLC

ISBN: 978-0-578-35477-4 (sc)

Library of Congress Control Number: 2022900192

Printed in the United States of America
First Printing 2022

"The hole in my heart is healing
the tears are slowly receding
The hope is melting away
The pain isn't here to stay.
It didn't work out as I planned
But now is the time to move on and stand
The world keeps going and I go too
A little bit stronger each day without you."

Katelyn Meithof

Dedication

I dedicate this book to my grandchildren and great-grandchildren as they are the future ambassadors of the next generation. I encourage them to create a world of kindness and love without discrimination.

Moving On From Life's Challenges

Moving on From Life's Challenges is based on a true story that took Mindy Briggs, a New York state native, from two failed marriages, through a miscarriage, past breast cancer, into an unexpected suicide of a friend, and to the loss of loved ones. All of this taking place over several years of her life to where she was finally able to put it all down on paper and painfully share it with the world.

Throughout the pain and many disappointments she was facing, Mindy, with each heartbreak, felt as though it was like putting a puzzle together: always trying to figure out how the complicated pieces somehow fit into her life.

She began to realize, little by little, the insights that were being revealed to her. The puzzle began to take shape, and Mindy could finally see the big picture of why every negative situation truly can have a positive outcome.

THIS IS HER STORY.

Contents

Chapter 1

Every Negative Has A Positive

At the age of 64, I have learned a lot about life through my experiences. One thing I have learned, in particular, is that whatever bad situation I was dealing with throughout the years ended up transforming me into a better person. If I hadn't experienced these hardships, I would never have become the strong, positive woman I am today.

The stories I am about to share with you are true. My purpose for putting my life story out there is to prove my point, that every negative has a positive, and to maybe help someone else along the way.

I have learned to live through the bad experiences, accept them, but do not remain in them, learn from them, and become stronger. That has become the motto by which I live every day.

Chapter 2

One Step Forward, Three Steps Back

I grew up in a small town in upstate New York. We lived on a quiet street in a middle-income neighborhood. Mom and Dad worked hard to take care of my brother, myself, and my two sisters. We were latch-key kids during the week, which meant our parents were still at work when we got home from school. We each had a key, latch-key, to open the front door of our house. My older sister was in charge of us since she was the oldest at fifteen. My brother was already out of the house and in the military. He was ten years older than me, and I was the youngest.

I don't remember too many arguments between us siblings growing up; however, I'm sure there were some. Like whenever my sisters had friends over, they would tell me to go away. One time I remember them wanting to build a fort outside. They said if I helped, I could hang out with them. Something I'd learn to ignore in the future.

But for now, I pulled off all of my bed blankets to make the roof for the fort. When it was all done, my sisters and their friends would not let me come in. So I did what any smart-aleck kid would do. I took all my blankets back, and they had no roof. That was who I was back then.

Every weekend, my Mom and Dad and my sisters and I would drive out to visit my grandmother. She adopted my Mom when my Mom was a child. This woman was actually my Mom's aunt, but we called her Grandma since that was the role she had taken on after adopting my Mom. My grandmother's home was about thirty minutes away from where we lived, so it wasn't a long drive. My grandmother lived alone. She had a neat house with a lot of small rooms with sliding doors. We used to pretend they were elevators. She also had a spooky attic that we would play in sometimes. My grandmother would sit at the table smoking Kent cigarettes. She had three long-haired white cats who had the run of the house. My Dad despised going there, but he knew it was important to Mom at the time. I remember him getting up out of the chair with cat hair all over his shirt, cussing at the "damn cats," as he would put it. Even at a young age, I remember not being fond of my grandmother myself. When her neighbor would stop by, my grandmother would be all smiles. But as soon as her neighbor would leave, my grandmother would say how much she couldn't stand her. It was the two-facedness I didn't like.

Despite that, for some reason we all wanted to stay overnight at my grandmother's house on the weekends. My two sisters always got to stay. Whenever I asked if I could stay, my grandmother would always tell me that I couldn't. After several times of me asking to stay and being turned down, I finally confronted my Mom one time during our ride back home. I asked her why my sisters could stay, but I couldn't. My Mom turned around from the front seat and told me my grandmother never wanted her to have me. *Wow*, I thought, *how cruel*. My grandmother and I remained distant after that.

Years later, her neighbor called me saying my grandmother was in the hospital and wanted to see me. I told her I wasn't going to visit her. She couldn't believe I would say that. She reiterated that my grandmother was dying. Against my better judgment, I decided to go. I brought my grandmother a beautiful bouquet of yellow flowers, wondering what she would have to say to me after all these years. She wasn't able to talk much because she was on oxygen. The only thing she said was that the flowers were beautiful, nothing else. No, *"I care about you"*, I am sorry. Nothing. I didn't stay long. I remember walking out of that hospital room thinking that I could have had a relationship with her, but she just chose not to like me simply because she felt Mom and Dad had their hands full already with three kids. Another child would just add to their burdens and hers. That's just the way my grandmother saw things at the time and projected that onto me.

I know now what it must feel like to be an orphan. So cold. My grandmother died the next day. It's amazing how much we take away from our situations and how they mold us along the way. The situation with my grandmother made me feel much less of myself, but I knew my Dad and Mom loved me. That's what I was able to take with me from my relationship with my grandmother.

*The Negative: I resented my grandmother. I felt abandoned by her. I wanted to be loved equally as my siblings were, but I was not.

*The Positive: As a grandmother now myself, even though I don't live near my grandkids I am there for them. That includes my bonus grandchildren (Not my blood grandkids) and my great-grandchildren. I treat them all equally and am so grateful for each one of them.

Chapter 3

Growing UP

Growing up, I was a Daddy's girl. I admit to being spoiled. One time, I remember one of my sisters got this really neat paper umbrella at the store near where we lived. She wouldn't let me play with it, so I told her I was going to tell Daddy. He stated it was hers, and she bought it with her own money. *Not fair,* I thought. *I want one too.* I begged my Dad until I wore him down, and he let me get one that day. I played that card with my Dad many times, and he always gave in. Of course it wouldn't have been total satisfaction without sticking my tongue out at my sister as if saying *ha, ha.* Looking back on it now, I realize that it was no wonder my siblings weren't too fond of me. I thought at the time that they were treating me badly. As it turns out, I had treated them just as badly. Siblings!

But life had a way of bringing its own challenges and obstacles my way, even though at home, I had things my way. I struggled in school especially, math and English in high school. It was harder for me to grasp the academics than for the other kids. The kids in school had no problem reiterating your shortcomings and making you feel small. I used to be thin, thank God, because if I were overweight it would have been one more caveat they would have thrown at me.

I couldn't wait to graduate from high school and move on with my life. In the seventies, the mindset was to get married young and have kids with the promise your husband would take care of you for the rest of your life. At the time, it sounded like the perfect escape. I had dated the same guy throughout high school. He popped the question, and I said yes without hesitation. I was married a year after high school graduation and had a son. I was thrilled. I had it all, a husband who would take care of me for the rest of my life, a precious son, and a nice place of my own in which to live.

My husband and I agreed I would be a stay-at-home Mom. I made a lot of sacrifices at the time due to the lack of a second income. Most couples with children used pampers. I used cloth diapers. I cut coupons to save money at the grocery store and cooked most of the meals at home. I had an old '69 Chevy Impala I used for short runs to the store and back while my husband had a nice truck he drove back and forth to work.

As a stay-at-home Mom, I was grateful to have a lot of one-on-one time with my son. We went for walks every day. He loved playing with his matchbox cars with me and his imaginary friends, Two Shoe and Giddy. He was infamous for picking up worms and putting them in his pockets, only for me to find them when I did the laundry. My girlfriend had bought him a Navy uniform he loved to wear and hated to take it off. She picked him up one day, along with her niece, to take them horseback riding at a place for kids. On the way home, I guess he had a moment of anger, and he bit the little girl's nose. I felt so bad. He was three at the time. Having no other siblings around at the time, I had to teach him some rules about not biting others. Having spent so much time with him, I knew when he was upset and when he was generally tired. He was like my best friend, only pint size. When my son was five and started school, I picked up a temporary retail job at the mall in Colonie Center for extra money for Christmas. I only worked hours during the time my son was in school, so it worked out well.

Wednesday evenings were our date nights to go bowling with our friends. One Wednesday evening, I was not able to attend because of work. We planned on bowling the following Wednesday night, but there was a bad snowstorm predicted. I thought it best I stay home with our son rather than drag him out in a dangerous blizzard. My husband decided to go bowling without me anyway, which was fine. He kissed me on his way out the door and told me he would be home directly after bowling.

I went to bed around eleven o'clock. I was tired. I woke up at five am. I realized my husband was not in bed. I checked throughout the house, but he was not there, so I looked in the driveway. There was a lot of snow, and it was blowing hard. I could barely open the door. His car was not in the driveway, he was not home. I panicked. I called his family and the friends we normally bowled with. I thought, *What should I do?* No one had seen him after bowling. *He had to have been in an accident somewhere.* I feared the worst.

Three hours later, still nothing. My next-door neighbor at the time stated he had seen Ken drive by his house an hour earlier. None of this was making any sense to me. His whole family came to our house. I called where I worked and told them I would not be at work that day but did not explain why.

Around noon my husband arrived at home. I ran out, so excited to see that he was okay, only for him to tell me he had to talk to me. But he didn't want to talk until the next day. I decided to let him have some time with his family at our house.

I drove down to my Mom and Dad's house and asked if my son and I could stay over. I told them I would go back up by myself the next morning and find out what was going on with my husband.

When I drove back home the next morning, the house was dark. It was around seven in the morning, and my husband should have been awake by now. I walked to the bedroom only to trip near the bed on some clothing lying on the floor. I turned on the light and saw my best girlfriend laying in our bed with little to no clothes on. I admit to losing it. I cussed them both out, screaming, and finally left. I was totally devastated.

It was three days before Christmas. *How could this have happened?* I was blindsided. I never saw this coming. We were not arguing or having issues at that time.

My husband refused to give me an explanation other than to say he wanted a divorce to be with her, the one I had thought of as a friend.

He said he wanted our son, Lou, and I to move out of the house. He wanted us to move out so he could be with my girlfriend there in MY home. As a stay-at-home Mom, where did he think we would be able to go? I had no outside job other than a part-time Christmas help at Sears in Colonie, NY. It was 1983. I will admit it was a tough time in my life but wait, there was much more strife to follow. My bad times didn't end there. It seemed they were only beginning.

I went back down to my Mom and Dad's house. By then, my Mom had gotten my son on the bus and off to school. I explained everything that had happened between Ken and me to my Mom. She told me to march back up there and tell **them** to leave. I did just that, and they did indeed leave my house. I didn't think it was possible, but that's when everything really started to go downhill.

My Mom called me a few days later telling me that my Dad had had a severe heart attack. She said he would be okay with bed rest. I decided I would handle my situation myself due to my Dad's health condition. Of course, the bills didn't stop coming. I was only bringing home fifty dollars a week at my part-time job. What was I going to do?

I immediately went to my supervisor, wanting to get full-time work. He reminded me that I was only hired as a temp, and the job was nearing an end in January. He had nothing for me. I lost it and started crying. He wanted to know what was going on. I told him my current circumstances, and he told me to give him two weeks. He promised he would find something full-time for me during that time.

In the meantime, I went back to work. I was feeling relieved, hoping he would keep his word. The day was finally over, and I went to the desk I kept my purse in, only to find out it was gone. I thought at first that I had just forgotten and left it elsewhere due to all I had on my mind. But nope, someone had stolen it. It was gone. In the meantime, I had no car keys, so no car to get me home. A nice guy from the auto department said he would hotwire my car so at least I could get home. But the car had a locking steering column, so it didn't matter that he could start it, I wouldn't be able to drive it. It was useless, but I had to get home. I bit the bullet and called my husband to see if he had an extra key. He did. He brought it to me that evening at work and quickly left without saying a word. All of the things my husband had taken care of in regard to the house now seemed to be my sole responsibility. He seemed to have disappeared into thin air. I called his work only to be told I was not to speak with him. I was not okay with that. I was still his wife, and Lou was still his son. One evening after work, I drove to Ken's work and told him I needed money. He gave me five dollars. One more slap in the face! I took it anyway, though. I needed it. The bill collectors had been calling. I was stalling them as long as I was able.

We had a long driveway that went from the side of the house all the way down to the street. The wind often took advantage of this long driveway and carried the snowdrift up towards the house and halfway down to the street. That made the snow deep and difficult to drive through. I would normally leave the car at the end of the driveway, so I didn't get blocked in. Of course, my husband had left us the 'shit' car that was on its last leg. I say the 'shit' car, on the contrary, it was my lifesaver. It had four bald tires, a broken windshield, and no muffler, that's how much my life needed saving at the time.

During that time, the car inspection was due. In the state of NY, cars had to have a yearly checkup to make sure they were road-worthy. The guy at the automotive place said that the car wouldn't pass the inspection. It has a broken frame and a lot of other, smaller issues. I literally begged him to pass it. I told him my situation. He said it was totally against his better judgment and he could get in a lot of trouble for this. He walked back to the car and placed the updated sticker on it. I won't state where that happened, but I was truly grateful since getting a ticket would have cost me money I did not have at that time.

And things just continued to escalate downhill from there. I was getting collection calls daily. My husband was not returning my calls. I was having trouble just affording food for me and my small son. It was below zero out for several weeks that January. I was getting five gallons of kerosene at a time for heating and cooking, but that quickly ran out because it was so cold. My water pipes froze and burst. A neighbor kindly helped get that taken care of for me. *This just can't get any worse*, or so I thought.

I contacted the public assistance in my town for help with food. I thought if I could get help with money for food, maybe I could start paying some of the other bills. But I was told I was making too much money to qualify. I reiterated that I was only bringing home fifty dollars a week, and I promised the assistance would only be temporary. They told me that the only way they would help me was if I quit my job and went on welfare. I felt that was degrading after all I had been through. Besides, I thought, wouldn't it make more sense to help someone short term with food as opposed to giving someone everything they need long term, that way they could help themselves and improve their lives? I told them to kiss my ass. I wasn't going on welfare. I was able to buy peanut butter, milk, eggs, and bread. When that ran low. I chose not to eat and fed my son. We were getting by, well sort of, the best we could.

I felt like such a failure though thinking that I couldn't even provide for my son. How could my husband just desert us like this? At the time I had a lot of resentment. For about three months, I had no idea where my husband and girlfriend were living. No one in town would tell me, or maybe they didn't know either. I would wait until my son was asleep and stand in front of the bathroom mirror and pretend I was talking to them and telling them just how much I hated both of them for doing such a cruel thing to us. As crazy as that sounds, it made me feel better. And then of course my mind would return back to why. *Why did this happen?* I thought all was well with our marriage. *Where did things go wrong?* I was never given an explanation as to why only that he wanted her instead of us.

One Saturday evening, after I paid whatever bills I could, I ended up with five dollars to last for the following week. I knew that was not going to work, and I refused to ask my parents, especially with Dad's condition, although he was back at home and improving. I also didn't want to ask my siblings for money as we were not all that close. I felt this was my problem, and I had to fix it somehow. I brought my son with me to church on Sunday. When the collection plate came around, I placed the whole five dollars in the plate, cried to myself, and asked God to help us.

After church, I went home and started a load of laundry, second-guessing my decision to give up the last five dollars we had. As I was unloading the clothes from the dryer, twenty dollars popped out. To this very day, I have no idea where that came from. I certainly did not have twenty dollars to my name. It had to have been stuck in there from when my husband had done laundry before he left us. I felt at that moment that God had heard my prayer. It wasn't a lot, but it was more than five dollars, and it totally got us through the next week. That day I stopped worrying about life and started believing in my heart that we would be fine.

I finally received a call back from my supervisor at Sears. He said, "I found a full-time job for you." "Really," I said. He asked me, "What do you know about accounting?" "Shoot, nothing," I honestly replied to him. He said, "Well, that's what you're going to be doing." He told me where to go and what time to meet. It was still at the same Sears store where I had been working. It was the first time in weeks that things were looking up. But now I would need a babysitter. Child care was not cheap. I knew whatever money I earned, I would have to turn over to someone to care for my son while I was at work, and I'd still be in a bad situation.

I had a girlfriend who lived two houses up from me. I decided to talk to her and see if she knew anyone who could help me with child care for a reasonable price. She came up with the best idea ever. She said, "I'll tell you what. You don't work weekends. How about I take your son after school every day, and you watch my kids on the weekend? No money would need to be exchanged." It was the perfect solution. I felt so blessed.

*The Negative: I was blindsided not only by my husband but also by my girlfriend. I had to muster up the courage every morning just to get out of bed and keep going. I had to create myself into a different person in front of my son, acting like I've got this when I really didn't.

*The Positive: Just as the cold winter turns into spring and nicer weather, that winter and the situation didn't last forever. Once things began to improve I felt I had learned a significant lesson about myself. I was stronger after all the turmoil had taken place. I will never forget what happened. I took away a lot of knowledge from that situation about trust, the goodness of others and to depend on myself.

Chapter 4

Divorce

I ended up getting divorced even though I didn't want to be in this situation. Our house was for sale, but I remained there for a while. My husband wanted to marry my girlfriend, the one he cheated on me with previously. We went to court and settled on the custody of our son. The child support he had to pay was only twenty-five dollars a week. My ex-husband and I decided on our own what custody we wanted for our son. I had custody the majority of the time. I was glad he actually wanted to see our son, but I was still upset and unsure of the effects that would have on our son then and in the future.

I felt it was time to get out of dodge for a while. I wasn't ready to run into my ex-husband and my girlfriend, and with all of us living in the same small town, it would be hard to avoid them. I talked to my supervisor at work about transferring my job temporarily to get away. He understood, and I was placed with a job in Rhode Island for two months. I had gotten a small apartment not far from where I would be working. I was thrilled at the opportunity to be elsewhere. I had been in this situation long enough. My son was happy to go with me. His only concern at the time was he wanted to stay in the same school. It wasn't going to be a problem because my job was only for the summer. The only problem I really had was the fact that I was still driving that '69 Chevy Impala. Even though at this point, I was making more money, I didn't want to purchase a new car just yet. I decided to risk it and wait until I had more income. My ex-husband took our son while I did the move. I loaded up the car and headed down the Massachusetts Turnpike.

All was going well. I was listening to the radio, which was another plus of the car that the radio was actually still working. As I was driving, I was singing away like I didn't have a care in the world when it started to cloud up and rain. Not just a little rain, but a major downpour. The exits on the Mass Pike are few and far between as everyone that has ever driven it knows. All of a sudden the driver's side windshield wiper completely blew off my car. It was now scraping metal to glass. What was amazing was, I was right in front of an exit near a gas station when that happened. Thankfully, I was able to get a new wiper and move on. I was so grateful it happened at that perfect time or, I would have had to stop and pull off the road until the rain stopped.

I arrived at the apartment, and even though I knew I had my work cut out for me, it was so peaceful. I felt like a huge weight had been lifted off my shoulders. Once I had everything moved in, I decided to take a cruise around and find the place where I would be working. I noticed my back tire on the driver's side was low on air, so I stopped at a gas station near the apartment. A nice guy came out and filled the tire with air for me. Little did I know he and I would become fast friends due to my car issues.

I located my new temporary employment and then drove back to my apartment. I decided to take a walk around. It was not like the small town I had just left. It was busier, more traffic, more like the suburbs. I headed back to my apartment and ran into a woman who introduced herself to me. She told me she was living in the same apartment complex. I didn't explain to her my circumstances, only that I would be there for a short time. She stated I should check out the beach and Block Island while I was there. I told her my son would be joining me and asked if she knew any places for childcare. She said she didn't have children and couldn't help me in regard to that. I only had a week to find childcare to take care of Lou while I would be working.

I started scouring the newspaper. There were several ads for childcare places. Going down the list, I was not impressed. One person had taken on several kids and lived on the main highway with no fence. Another one wanted way too much money. I finally found one who I had a good gut feeling about for some reason. She was a mom of three kids near my son's age, she homeschooled her children, and her Mom lived at her home to help oversee all the kids. I went to check it out. At first glance, I was impressed with her home. It was beautiful and clean.

She stated the kids do not sit around nor do they watch tv. They make crafts and bake, and they stay busy. She had an above-ground swimming pool for them to swim in also. Basically, she would interact with them all day. Her kids were as polite and kind as I found her to be. Perfect. I felt very confident about them watching my son. One more check off my list.

I continued to unpack and set up the apartment and get ready for my son to arrive on the weekend. I waited outside for Lou. I couldn't wait to see him. He came all smiles and happy. He couldn't wait to show me what he brought me from New York. It was a small box and in it was a frog. Unfortunately, it was a very dead frog. He felt bad. He thought it would survive the trip and it would be fun to have a new pet. I told him I appreciated the gesture. I told him maybe we could find a Rhode Island frog for a pet.

I wanted to take my son and introduce him to where he would be staying while I was at work. I set up a meeting, and it all went as planned. I was so happy that all went well, and he felt comfortable there. The weekend seemed to fly by. I was ready for work and ready to take him to Carly's house for the day to spend with her kids. When I went to get in the car, I noticed that the same tire was losing air again. I thought I better stop and get that tire filled first. Out came the same gentleman to help me put air in it again. I thanked him, and we moved on.

My son was adjusting to our new surroundings, and so was I. The job was exactly what I was doing in NY, and the people I worked with were nice. I stopped at the gas station every morning for a coffee, and the attendant would make sure my tires were in order. Coming here was such a good decision for us. We were free from all the sad and unhappy moments we had been dealing with and back to being us. We never got to Block Island, but we did take a bus and go to the beach. It was awesome.

The two months seemed to just fly by. Before we knew it, it was time to head back to New York, and I felt we were both ready to face the inevitability of going back to the small town. My son would be starting school soon, and I had to get back to my job in NY.

The escape to Rhode Island had been perfect. Sometimes you have to run away to reevaluate your next chapter of life and where you go from there. Going back to NY was hard, but not as hard if I hadn't taken the time to reflect and realize I could be happy again, perhaps elsewhere one day.

*The Negative: I hated the fact I was now divorced. I kept my son away from all his friends and family for two months and left him with good people to look after him although I hadn't known them previously. We had no family there nor did we know anyone where we were staying.

*The Positive: It was a very pleasurable getaway. Lou and I were able to spend one on one time together and laugh and be ourselves again. The two months away gave me the courage to be able to go back and face the situation with a better mindset.

Chapter 5

Marriage #2

A few years after all the dust had settled from the divorce from my initial marriage, I felt ready to date again. A girl from high school had contacted me wanting to know if I wanted to go on a blind date with a farmer. Ah no, I had told her right away. She said he was really cute, but I knew what that meant. She kept trying to convince me, but I kept telling her no. She asked me to meet her for a drink at a local pub one night, and I agreed. As we were chatting and catching up on our lives, a gorgeous man approached our table, and she introduced us. He was the farmer, Chris. He walked away after the introductions were politely made. My girlfriend explained that this was the guy she wanted me to meet. Wow, I just changed my mind about farmers!

She had Chris come back to the table, and she conveniently left. He had also been divorced but had no children. He was polite as well as handsome, and we had a great conversation. He asked me out on a date. I figured it was safe knowing my girlfriend recommended him. I told him I was divorced and had a son, and we would have to wait until he was at his Dad's for the weekend.

On our first date, we went to a local restaurant in town. Chris couldn't stray far due to having ties to the farm. He and his Dad ran the farm by themselves. They owned a dairy farm and milked 130 cows every day, twice a day. I was very taken in not only by this man's looks but also his demeanor. We continued dating, and I was on cloud nine. Chris was a hard worker, and it showed in his muscular physique. He could have easily been doing commercials for expensive colognes or jeans. As time passed, he wanted to meet my son. I talked to my son about it since I thought it important for him to be part of the decision-making about this issue. At this time, Lou was around eight years old, had a good head on his shoulders, and had good people sense. Lou was fine with meeting Chris. We all decided to go roller skating. We had a great time. My son thought Chris was a great guy. After three months of dating, Chris asked me to marry him. I thought it was quick but couldn't help thinking how great it would be for my son to experience farm life as much as I would enjoy it, and I would have a great partner too. The farm Chris and his father had was close to town from where I lived.

During the time we were dating, I had introduced Chris to my parents. Mom had us over for dinner several times, and we always had a good time. My Mom and Dad thought he was great as well. Chris asked my dad for permission to marry me, and my dad gave him his blessing. My parents were probably glad to see me happy again after all I had been through during my first marriage.

Chris' family was a little mismatched. His Mom was divorced from his Dad, and she was married to a nice guy, although I thought they seemed like two opposites. His Dad was outspoken and was married to a woman I didn't really care for, but I wasn't marrying them, so it didn't really matter. Or so I thought. Chris also had a younger brother who was very fun to be around and was married, with two young girls.

A lot was going on at the time like it is with planning any wedding. While we were riding around trying to cinch up plans, we came across an old church at the top of a hill on a dirt road in the middle of nowhere. It was near the farm. I asked Chris to stop so we could check it out. We walked in, and it smelled old like maybe there had been many services and weddings there back in the day. We could tell from the smells and how it looked that the little church had a history. It was like going back in time. I loved it. I asked Chris what he thought of the idea of us getting married there, and he said it was a good idea. I knew it would be a perfect setting. Part of his honey-do list was to find out if they were still holding services there and whom to contact about our wedding plans.

In between all the chaos of planning the wedding, I realized we would be moving to another town which meant my son would have to change schools. I didn't want to do that, nor did he. I contacted his school and asked them if Lou could continue there, and they said he could because his dad was paying taxes in that school district. They stressed that I would have to make sure to get Lou to school every day as there were no busses to transport him from where we were moving to on the farm. It would work out perfectly since I had to go right by his school on my way to work and could also pick him up on the way home.

One evening when we were having dinner with his Dad and stepmom, I told them about the school issue and how I was able to resolve it. His stepmom stated it was stupid, and that Lou needed to go to the school district he would be living. I told her that Lou wanted to remain in his current school, and it wouldn't be a problem. She continued until I got upset and let her know, without reservation, that he was my son and not hers. It was my decision, not hers. Unfortunately, we didn't get off to a good start, but I stood my ground, and Chris agreed with me, which helped.

Looking back on things now, this was a red flag. I never saw the red flags though, because I was caught up with trying to move on with my life and just be happy after all I had been through.

I knew a photographer from work who agreed to take the pictures at our wedding. He showed me photos he had taken of other weddings. Everything was falling into place. I had the dress picked out and sized, and I had my sisters as bridesmaids. My brother played guitar and was going to entertain at the reception at the local town hall, which was not far from the church where we would be married. My Mom and Dad were to do the catering. Everything was set.

The evening before the wedding, Chris's brother planned a bachelor party for him. I didn't care. I had plenty to do the prior evening. Early the next morning, I went to the farm to pick up some items I needed that I had left behind and noticed Chris was still in bed. I said, "Hey sleepyhead, it's our wedding day, get up." He rolled over and said, "I got married yesterday." He reeked of alcohol. I thought, *oh my god, now what.*

I called his brother wanting to know what the hell happened last night. He said that they all drank too much. I reminded him, as best man, it was his responsibility to get Chris to the church on time. I was upset. I couldn't understand why they didn't have his bachelor party on a different night.

My girlfriend, Marie, and her date at the time came to pick me up to take me to the church. I told her on the ride there that I thought I was making a big mistake. I wanted to cancel the whole thing. I was having second thoughts, for good reason, but how could I cancel at this point. Looking back again, another red flag.

Everything for the wedding was all set. I met my Dad at the back of the church, but he knew me like a book. I tried not to let on what I was thinking, but Dad said, "I am never walking you down the aisle again." I knew what he meant. He didn't want to see me getting another divorce. I didn't even know if Chris' brother had gotten him to the church. When I walked up the aisle on my Dad's arm, thankfully, Chris was standing there at the altar waiting for me. I looked over at his brother, the best man, standing there with a big black eye. I just shook my head. As the day progressed, I let it go and enjoyed the day. I thanked everyone for coming, and we headed out to Niagara Falls for our honeymoon. We seemed to be back on track with our relationship.

A couple of years had passed, and we all were enjoying farm life. I enjoyed baling hay, and my son was thrilled at being able to drive the tractors. I never realized what all was involved in farm life. It's hard work and yet a very peaceful way of life.

Chris had talked to me one evening in bed about how he wanted to start a family. I understood, even though we hadn't discussed it prior. We decided to start planning it. It wasn't long until I became pregnant. I had been pregnant before, but this didn't seem normal though. I was sick from the time I got up in the morning until I went to bed for two straight months. It felt like something wasn't quite right, but I wasn't sure what it could be. It was hard trying to work every day, but I mustered up the courage and kept going.

By now, my son had taken a shine to this guy so much that he wrote an essay at school about him. Lou was going to read the essay to everyone at an open house they were holding in a week on a Wednesday evening. I mentioned it to Chris, and I also notated it on the calendar. Prior to my pregnancy, Chris and I were in a volleyball league on Wednesday nights. I stopped going because I hadn't been feeling well. But Chris agreed to go to the open house to hear Lou's essay.

My son was so happy Chris was going to come and hear what he had written in his essay about him. I kept reminding Chris about the school event because I knew he had a lot going on with the farm, and I didn't want him to forget how important this was to my son. On the evening of the event, it was nearing the time for us to leave, and I told Chris that he needed to start getting ready so we would not be late. He looked at me and let me know he was going to play volleyball that night instead. I couldn't believe what I was hearing. I reminded him that he said he would go to the school. I pleaded with him and told him what a big deal it was for Lou, and it should be for him, too. Chris repeated that he was going to play volleyball. I was devastated. How could he do this? He promised he would go. Now I have to tell my son he reneged. I was so angry. Lou and I went, and when the teacher mentioned to my son about reading the essay, he declined. After it was over, I decided to take him out for ice cream. I tried to, somehow, smooth it over, but I knew how disappointed he was.

When I got home, I got Lou off to bed. It was ten o'clock. His room was off the bathroom. I had to use the bathroom before going to bed myself. (being pregnant does that to you) I felt something strange as I was using the bathroom and looked in the toilet. There was blood everywhere. I called out to Lou to see if he was still awake. Thankfully, he was. I asked him to get Chris for me. When Chris came in, I showed him all the blood, and he just told me to go to bed. WHAT? He asked me what I wanted him to do. I told him that this was not normal. I needed to go to the hospital. He let me know he was not going to take me to the hospital since it was already ten o'clock and for me to go to bed. I couldn't believe it. I went downstairs and called my sister to see if she would take care of my son while I drove myself to the hospital. I guess that made Chris feel like, at that point, he had to step up and take me. He did, and it was one very quiet ride might I add. When we arrived at the hospital, I went to stand up, and there was a big puddle of blood on my seat. I asked Chris to go in and get a wheelchair at which he refused. I had to walk into the hospital with blood running everywhere. I was so embarrassed. It was a Catholic hospital, and they were very accommodating. They put me in a bed in a private room. They were concerned about my blood loss and said they might have to give me a blood transfusion. When the doctor came in, he stated he would not be able to save the baby.

The doctor gave me a moment with my husband while he prepared for the D & C. I looked at my husband, and he let me know that he couldn't believe that I was unable to have this child. The one thing he wanted, and I couldn't even do this for him. I didn't even know what to say. I was shocked. There was no concern for my life or maybe saying that we could try again. Nope. He was ticked off that it didn't go as planned. When the nurse came in, he asked where he could get a cup of coffee, and he left. *God where does this shit end*, I thought. I cried the rest of the evening. I didn't plan to have a miscarriage. This was not my fault. Why is he blaming me for this? Is it me, or is it everyone I come in contact with loves to hurt me?

I don't remember the surgery, but I do remember a nurse sitting in a chair in my room facing me. She said I didn't wake up in recovery, so they wheeled me back to the room. She wanted to know how I was feeling. I told her I was ready to leave the hospital. She told me that my husband must love me so much since he sent me a beautiful bouquet of flowers. She told me she had the bouquet at the nurses' station. I told her, very unkindly to her, for my husband to take his flowers and shove them up his ass. Unfortunately, I forgot I was in a Catholic hospital. I thought she was going to have a coronary. I told her I was sorry, but she had no idea what had been going on. She told me she thought I needed counseling. I told her that I could care less about counseling. I needed to get out of there.

Chris came to pick me up, and I left the flowers for the nurses. I couldn't bring myself to take them home with me as a reminder of how Chris had treated me. The hospital had to supply me with scrubs to go home in because Chris didn't think to bring me anything to wear for the ride home.

This marriage was now a terrible situation for myself and my son. I was not about to live with a man who has no consideration for my son or me. I had to end it. I asked Chris for a divorce, to which he agreed. I think after losing the baby, he was as ready to end our marriage as I was. I was thankful for that at least.

I continued to feel like a failure. Divorced for the second time. What was I doing wrong to keep repeating these same situations with men? I was done. I told myself, never again.

My first ex-husband and his wife had two children of their own during the years. They were siblings of Lou's. Of course, there were birthdays and get-togethers where Lou and I needed to be present, like it or not, for all the kids. So we attended all the celebrations.

One day, I was at their home planning my son's senior graduation party from high school. It wasn't until that day, over coffee and conversation, that I realized my ex-husband and his new wife were far more compatible than he and I ever were when we were married. My ex-husband was smiling and joking and so was my ex-girlfriend. It was on that day I no longer had resentment towards them. I could finally let it go once and for all.

*The Negative: I was now divorced twice, not wanting to be, and single having many more responsibilities.

* The Positive: The situation taught me I was much stronger and capable of much more than I could have ever imagined. I had been searching for someone to make me happy instead of taking time and loving myself first. I learned to trust God and that there was a reason for that season of anger and sadness. I am no longer that girl who needs someone to take care of her. I am totally capable of taking care of myself, and although my son is my only son, he now has brothers he stays in touch with to share and exchange life experiences with.

Chapter 6

Family & Friends' Support During Grief

The one very positive aspect of my life after my second divorce was my son, Lou. He was my rock. Even on my absolute worst days, he used his uncanny humor to get me out of any bad mood I might have been in at the time. He seemed to know exactly what to say and the right time to say it. He would have me laughing uncontrollably, letting me forget about everything else that was going on in my life.

Lou was a good student at school as well as a good son for me at home. Years later, after Lou graduated from high school, he was off to the Navy. I was so proud of him and missed him immensely. It had been just him and me together for so long. I had to adjust to a new situation once again.

Lou's travels with the Navy brought him to many countries. He would send me pictures and letters from wherever he went, and I treasured each and every one of them. When he arrived back in the

US, he was stationed in the state of Washington. I was happy he was back safe.

During all of this time, my Mom had fallen sick. Dad was recuperating from his heart problems, and now she was diagnosed with ovarian cancer. She had also been struggling for years with arthritis. I remember her telling me one day at her house that she was sick of being sick. I cried with her. There was nothing I could do to make it better. I felt helpless.

My Mom had a hard life growing up. She was born in Germany and came to this country as a child. Her Mom and Dad later abandoned her. She never discussed that part of her life with me or any of my siblings. The reason for her parents abandoning her remained a mystery. My Mom lived with her aunt on her Mom's side here in the United States. My Mom and Dad met while he was on leave from the Army. My Dad's sister lived two houses from where my Mom lived in Schenectady, NY. My Mom frequently went to his sister's house to visit. There she met and eventually married my Dad.

Moving On From Life's Challenges

My Dad was a mechanic in the Army. He could fix any car or diesel engine. After the war, Dad worked at a Ford dealership as head mechanic. He played the harmonica and enjoyed beer and cigars in his downtime, which wasn't all that often as he took on side work in his garage working on friends' vehicles for extra money.

When I was in the second grade, I was in a play at school and was the main character. I was excited about being the lead in the play and worked very hard on my part. I asked both of my parents to come to see me in the play. But Mom and Dad both said they couldn't attend as it was in the middle of the day, and they both worked. I was so disappointed. I didn't understand why they couldn't come to see me in the play. Throughout the whole play, I kept looking in the audience, hoping they would show. But I didn't see them. When the play was finally over, there stood my Dad in all his greasy attire from work. I ran up and hugged him, grease and all. I was so happy he came. It meant a lot to me. That was a long time ago, but that memory still remains clear in my mind. It's what kids remember, the things you do with them. Not the stuff you buy for them, it's the love you give them, in whatever form it takes.

Mom had many talents. I remember she played the guitar and was very good at it. Dad would make a campfire in the backyard, and we all would sit around it. Mom would play and sing, and Dad would chime in on his harmonica as she played. She also was an amazing cook. My favorite was her sauerbraten. Sauerbraten is a traditional German roast of heavily marinated meat. It was about the only thing from my Mom's German ancestry she shared with me.

My Mom and I had many conversations over coffee about life, hers and mine when I was in my late twenties early thirties while I would visit my parents' house. We mostly talked about her life since moving to the US, not before. We discussed my marriages, my son, and my job. It always made me feel better after our times together.

I was devastated about my Mom's cancer news and decided to bring her brochures of Salem, MA. I knew she wanted to travel to see that city one day. When she was in the hospital, I told her I would take her there when she got out and was feeling up to it. She seemed happy about this and said she looked forward to it.

I received a call at work from one of my sisters a few days later stating Mom's condition had deteriorated. The doctors gave her just twenty-four hours to live. I couldn't believe it. The doctors had to be wrong. It was heartbreaking news. I was at the hospital with my Mom more than I was at home. My older sister arrived and convinced me to go home one night to get some rest, so I did. She called me at three o'clock in the morning and said that Mom had passed. I was so mad that I had left the hospital and had gone home. I should have stayed. I had a hard time accepting she was really gone. I never have forgiven myself for not being with her in her passing. Many years later, as I write this, I still tear up.

Our family had a small private service at my parents' house with a pastor I knew. Months passed, and I still couldn't wrap myself around all the grief of losing my Mother. If I could just communicate with her again, have a conversation with her like I used to, I knew it would help me cope with the situation.

My girlfriend, Marie, suggested I take psychic development classes with the chance that perhaps I could communicate with my Mother. Marie stated she would be glad to take them with me. I was on board immediately, another chance to communicate with my Mother, I had to try. But then I remembered I was a Lutheran Christian and knew that it was an inappropriate practice as a Christian to try to communicate with the dead. But still, I couldn't seem to dismiss the fact that it might help me heal from the loss of my Mother.

As time passed after my Mother's death, I was not feeling any better, so I decided to take Marie up on her offer of attending the psychic classes. It was such a healing experience for me. However, after two years of taking the classes, I did not hear anything from my Mom, but it definitely helped the healing process through the meditation practices I learned. It wasn't until years later Mom did communicate with me. It was quite amazing and in a strange and mysterious way that I could hardly believe.

*The Negative: My Mom passed away, and I missed her immensely.

*The Positive: She was given to me as my Mom for a long time, and she is no longer suffering.

Chapter 7

My First Airplane Flight

Lou called me one day and asked me to fly out to visit him while he was stationed at the Bremerton Naval Station in Washington State. He was there to decommission a submarine. He knew I didn't fly, and it would have taken me forever to drive. I tried to convince him to fly home instead, but he told me he did not have any leave time.

As we continued our conversation, he interrupted me. "Mom," he said, "just get on a plane and come out here." He said he had met a girl and wanted to marry her, but he wanted me to meet her first.

"Really? You don't need my approval," I responded to him.

"It's no big deal, Mom, you can fly. You get a ticket, go to the airport, and get on the plane."

"Okay," I said. "She must be pretty special."

He then handed the phone to his future fiancé. "Hi," she said. "My name is Dani." I asked her how they met. She told me that they met online. Then I wanted to know how long they had known each other. She said it had been just a few months. They were both in their late twenties. At that point, I wasn't concerned because my son didn't date a lot in high school. He spent a lot of time working and going to school. I know that was more important to him at the time than dating.

Dani then told me she wanted to give me the heads up that she had two children from a previous marriage, and would I be okay with that? I told her that was fine with me, and I wanted to know all about them.

I was excited to see my son again and to meet Dani, but I was still apprehensive about having to fly. I knew I had to do it, so I booked the flight as soon as I could. My first flight out of Albany, NY, was a connecting flight to Michigan, on a very small plane. It literally had about 20 seats. When I boarded, the pilot stated that everyone had to sit in the seats they were assigned because it could be too much weight on one side. *Are you kidding me?* It was very noisy, a turboprop plane I believe. The takeoff was okay, but I was not so happy with landing. I was nervous, and now I had to get off this plane and go on another flight. I couldn't believe it.

The next flight was delayed by two hours due to bad weather which put me into Washington State later that evening. Once in the air, there was a storm, and there was lightning all around the plane. They served coffee. All of a sudden there was a lot of turbulence. I had never experienced turbulence of course.

"Do you think we are going to crash?" I said to the woman sitting next to me.

She said, "No, it will be okay. It's normal. You don't fly much do you?"

"No", I said, "this is only my second flight." I tried to relax, but my white knuckles proved that It was hard to do.

When I got off the plane and walked into the airport terminal, I couldn't believe my eyes. There stood my son and future daughter-in-law holding a huge sign they had made. The sign said: '**Welcome Grandma Mindy,** and it had some balloons attached to it. It was so festive and made me feel so welcomed.

My son was holding a small boy in a carrier, and Dani's little girl was holding a small bouquet of flowers. After the hugs and cries, Dani introduced me to Bryce, her son, two years old, and Nicole was four. Nicole handed me the flowers and said, "These are for you." She then immediately put up her little arms for me to pick her up. We bonded right away. It was a great evening.

We spent several days getting acquainted and catching up. Dani, at the time, was going to nursing school. My son had a few hours to spend with the kids and me. We all cleaned the house while Dani was at school. We thought we would surprise her. My son picked up tickets to a Mariners baseball game for us all to go to that weekend. The Mariners won, and we had a great time. While we were there, I called my nephew, who lived in Oregon, and we all met in Seattle for dinner. It was nice having a relaxing visit with old and new family.

Several months later, they were stationed in Florida for military training for Lou. Lou and Dani were married in November of 1999 at a beautiful ceremony in Monticello, near Tallahassee. It was a unique wedding. They arrived at a beautifully decorated gazebo in a wooded setting by horse and carriage. The weather was perfect, and after the ceremony, the reception was held in a barn they had magically transformed for just such occasions. Soon after the wedding, my son adopted Nicole and Bryce. They were a complete family, finally.

They then were stationed in St. Mary's, Georgia, for a few years. I was braver at flying by then and would visit during the winter. My daughter-in-law would pick me up when I flew into the Jacksonville airport. We would do some shopping, and then we would drive an hour back to their place in Georgia. I loved the area. I felt so comfortable there. It had a more city atmosphere. Not like NY where everyone knew your business. You'd be lucky to run into someone twice unless you chose to. It intrigued me. I knew deep down that I wanted that one day. I not only hated leaving them, but I also hated leaving the area. I loved Jacksonville. It was beautiful.

Several months later, Lou and Dani told me they received orders to upstate New York. I was thrilled. When I wasn't working, I spent as much time as I could with Nicole and Bryce. They are such great kids. We did a lot of sleepovers. We went on bike rides, night walks around Cobleskill, and went swimming when the weather cooperated.

I used to take the kids for rides, and we would sometimes stop and get something to eat. Their parents didn't allow them to eat in the car, write on the windows, or draw pictures on the glass of the car when it frosted over, but grandmas usually turn a blind eye to such things. When the children wanted money for something, I would give them things to do to earn it so they would appreciate the money and not think they could take advantage of my good nature.

One time, I told them I would give them each five dollars to clean my car, and clean it, they did. I gave them the cleaning supplies for the job. When they came back with an empty can of Armour All, I was concerned. I walked out to see their work. Just as I expected, my car shined from the Armour All.

It was everywhere you could imagine. It looked absolutely beautiful. I had to have a death grip on the steering wheel to be able to drive it, but they did as I asked. They cleaned my car!

As time went on, even though I was enjoying my family being here, I couldn't stop thinking about moving. It was nearing September of 2003, and I knew winter was soon on its way. I talked to Lou and Dani about my thoughts of moving. I reasoned with them that they were in the military, and they won't be staying here permanently either. They understood and gave me their blessing.

*The Negative: My son was marrying Dani with two young children only after knowing and dating her for a few months.

*The Positive: I connected with Dani, and I knew by the kids' demeanor she would be a great Mom if they were ever to have kids together. I loved the kids and now instantly had a larger family.

Chapter 8

Wanting to Live The Dream

In September 2003, at the age of 46, I decided to leave upstate New York to relocate to Jacksonville, Florida. I decided I no longer cared to shovel out another winter season in the northeast.

I planned for months how to take on this trip. Whenever I had a free moment, I would get online, and I would go to the Florida Chamber of Commerce website to get information. Since I didn't know anyone in Florida, nor did I have a job lined up, or the exact location, I used this website to help me. I just knew I wanted to live in Jacksonville. It's difficult trying to get things in order when you don't actually live there. I saved the three months of money I felt I needed to get things started in my new state. I knew I would need money to travel there, gas, food, lodging, and I would need money once I got there until I found a job. I placed all my belongings that would not fit in my car into storage. I planned to go back for them later.

I love to camp, so I decided on the way down to tent it on good days and hotel it on rainy days. It took several days driving from New York to Florida. I wasn't in a rush and wanted to enjoy the drive and the stops along the way. I remember stopping at a campground in South Carolina to tent it for the evening. When I checked in, the woman at the desk was concerned about why I would camp alone. I didn't think anything of it and told her It would be fine. I had no idea until I had to continue driving for about two miles on a desolate dirt road. It felt like I was in the middle of nowhere. That's when I realized why she was concerned. Literally, anything could have happened out there, and it would have been a while before anyone would have known. Nothing happened, thankfully. I actually slept well and was back on the road early the next morning.

When I finally approached the sign that said **Welcome to Florida**, I was ecstatic. I did it! Immediately after that, I got scared. I thought, *What if I don't get a job? What if it doesn't work out?* I had no intention of driving back. I **had** to make it work.

Moving On From Life's Challenges

I arrived at a campground called Hanna Park on my first night in Jacksonville, Florida. I hadn't planned on this particular campground, but it looked like the perfect place for me at the time. I chose to stay in a cabin at their facility. Across from my cabin, in a travel trailer, was an elderly couple who introduced themselves to me. They were hired, by the campground owners, to oversee the grounds and help other campers.

The couple noticed that my license plate was from New York, and they asked who I came to Florida to visit. I told them I didn't have any relatives or know anyone in Florida, nor did I have a job. When I explained why I had driven there, they looked at me like I was crazy. The woman said, in her quaint, charming southern voice, "Honey, you need to drive back to New York." She spent about a half-hour trying to convince me to go back. I told her that was not my plan.

The woman started to walk away and said, "If there is anything I can do to help, let me know." I said, "Do you have a phone book and know the area well?"   Shortly after, she appeared back with a telephone book in hand. She was helpful with getting me information and directions. The first thing I did was try to get a PO box at the Post Office. Everyone I went to, had no mailbox available. They told me to go to the UPS store and get a temporary box until a Post Office box became available. I did. It was more expensive, but in the long run, it was great because it had an actual address tied to it and not a PO Box since basically I was kind of homeless. I located the employment agency and returned every day. Within two weeks, I had a job using the phony address as my location. I was detailing newly constructed homes in Orange Park. Not my dream job, but employment, nonetheless.

In order to keep moving on, I kept returning to the Workforce Employment Agency looking for evening employment. Walmart had an opening for an evening accountant job. I applied and got the job. However, I was still struggling with a place to live. A coworker of mine just happened to hear I needed a place, and she was looking for a roommate to help her with expenses. We got along well, and she had a nice place. I told her it would be temporary until I could find a place of my own.

Florida was all new to me. For one thing, I knew nothing about hurricanes. There were four hurricanes to hit Florida that year, one I remember in particular, Hurricane Francis. At her place, I was in my room on the computer researching the next storm. I was nervous about the oncoming storm, then out of the corner of my eye, I saw this little piece of paper slide under my door. It was a handwritten note from my roommate stating: "Hurricane party tomorrow night, dinner & drinks will be served. Don't miss it!" *Wait, what? People have parties when a hurricane is coming.* I thought that was so bizarre, but I quickly realized that it is quite common for residents in Florida here to have hurricane parties. The reason being individuals pool their resources with the expectation there will be no electricity and no open stores or restaurants for several days. She invited several people to the house during the storm for her hurricane party. It was really fun and totally helped ease my mind. We all weathered the storm that night with no incidents or power outages.

As time went by, working two jobs was getting old pretty quickly. It was now October 2004. I went back to the Workforce Employment Agency and happened to see a posting for a full-time accounting job at the Sawgrass Marriott in Ponte Vedra. I thought, *What could it hurt to check it out?* I filled out an application while I was there, and low and behold, two days later, they scheduled an interview.

I was instructed to drive up to the main entrance and meet in the Human Resource Office. I soon realized this wasn't just some hotel. It was where the PGA golf tournament was held every March. When I pulled up, the valet wanted my keys. I stated I was only there for a job interview. He said that they don't charge for interview parking. I felt the job interview went well. I had total confidence when I left. I felt I had a good shot at the job. Two weeks passed, and I heard nothing. I called to reinforce my interest in the job only to be told they were still interviewing.

Three weeks passed, and still nothing. I called again, and they stated they were waiting for the budget review. Four weeks later, I called again, and it was down to three possible candidates, including myself. The next day I received a call that I had the job. Hallelujah! Now I only had to work one job.

I loved the job and the people. My supervisor was very professional and personable. She and I sometimes spent time outside of work for lunch or dinner. We got to know each other quite well and formed a close friendship.

Her husband was in a band and was also a band teacher for a local school. She constantly tried to get me to go out with them and hear his band play at a local venue called the Sun Dog Diner. I would decline every time because I lived in Orange Park, which is quite far from Jacksonville Beach, where he and his band played. I wasn't fond of driving late at night or hanging out at a bar.

One Saturday evening, she finally convinced me, and I told her I would go to hear them. I remember taking a long leisurely walk that day in the park. When I got back, I was tired and thinking of calling my supervisor to let her know I was not coming. But I didn't feel that was the right thing to do.

My roommate was all excited and said, "I have a great outfit you can wear. Let's do your makeup, and who knows, maybe you will meet a great guy." "Trust me," I told her, "you don't meet great guys in a bar, nor am I interested in meeting anyone anyway." I ended up barely wearing makeup and just clipping my hair up. I threw on my flip-flops and headed out the door. I did not care what I looked like that evening whatsoever.

When I arrived at the Sun Dog Diner, I could hear the band playing from where I parked. Wow, I couldn't believe it. They sounded so great. Her husband played the Saxophone and keyboard at the same time, a talented guy. I was enjoying the evening when across the bar, I noticed a gentleman staring at me. I kept trying to avoid eye contact. It wasn't five minutes, and over he strutted and introduced himself with a cigar in hand. "Hi, my name is Jimmy." I continued to reinforce my non-interest. He kept pursuing. At that point, my supervisor began to get concerned.

"Do you want me to have my husband talk to this guy?" She could see the troublesome look on my face. "No," I said. He then proceeded to tell me he was a car salesman, which only incarcerated him more. I figured if I kept avoiding him, he would go away.

The next thing out of Mr. Car Salesman was, "You are the prettiest girl in this place." "Really?" I said sarcastically. Nice try, but no cigar! I thought. He eventually ended up wearing me down until I gave him my phone number. That's something I would never have done. I guess persistence pays off. He walked me to my car that night, and I left, only for him to call me as I was still driving on the way home.

We communicated not dating for several months off and on. One evening, he invited me over for dinner. He was going to grill out. I told him it wasn't a good night. The apartment I shared with my coworker only had one bathroom, and we chose to initiate bathroom times. That was my shower evening time. I told him about that, at which his response was for me to take a shower at his place.

My first thought was, Is this a safe thing to do? I told him I did not feel comfortable about that. He said that he would change his plans and pick up a pizza while I took my shower. I agreed. He kept his word and did leave. He also left a glass of wine on the counter for me. When he arrived back with the pizza, we had a wonderful chat, and he was a total gentleman and never tried anything. I was impressed, and there were more dates to follow.

He lived over on Southside Boulevard. We would get together occasionally in between his hectic car salesman job and my job at Sawgrass. Several months later, he asked about us moving in as friends. I felt it might be a good idea. At that point, I knew I could trust him, and it was a half-hour closer to my work.

*The Negative: I left my good friend and roommate, who was very upset with me even though I gave her a month's notice to find another roommate. She had been dating someone who I was not comfortable being around since he had a criminal background.

*The Positive: My intuition told me it was time to move on with another chapter of my life. I was looking forward to spending more time with Jimmy in between our hectic jobs.

Chapter 9

Cancer Arrives Unexpectedly

Life was going well for about three months, but one thing I noticed was I was always falling asleep early. I couldn't figure it out because I've always been active. I would come home from work, fall asleep around six pm, and wake up at seven the next morning, never having had dinner. Jimmy would come home late from work, so he never even actually noticed. Then one morning, while taking a shower, I noticed a lump in my right breast. I really didn't panic or anything but was concerned enough to schedule an appointment at Salisbury Imaging just to make sure it wasn't anything serious. They did the typical mammogram at the end of May 2005. They stated they would let me know if there was an issue.

I didn't hear anything back from the doctor, nor did I call. I thought, *No news is good news*. It was now the end of August 2005. Jimmy came in early one night with the mail and handed me a letter from the doctor's office where I had the mammogram at Salisbury Imaging. The letter said they wanted to do a follow-up visit. Okay, I thought. I still wasn't all that concerned. Other than being tired, I wasn't having any issues.

One week later, I was given a referral to an OBGYN to schedule a stereotactic biopsy. I had an appointment the following day. Of course, every doctor I had to see charged me a copay. When I met with the OBGYN doctor, she told me to find a surgeon. That was the extent of her help. She really didn't do anything but waste my time off work to go there as she could have given me the information over the phone.

Two days later, I found a surgeon and went in for another appointment, and yet another copay. He reviewed my mammograms with me and stated I had bilateral masses in both breasts. He scheduled more mammograms and a second opinion from the radiologist with no mentioning of a biopsy. My insurance company denied this because I did not have a primary doctor at the time. One day later, I found a primary doctor to see me and another copay, the primary doctor then gave permission to the surgeon to follow up with his request for a second opinion.

Ah, yes, so the medical maze began.

Prior to the appointment for the actual biopsy that the surgeon was going to perform, I was asked to pick up my previous mammograms that were taken at Salisbury Imaging.

That meant more time off work. When I arrived back at the surgeon's office with my films, they stated during transport in my car, they had gotten overheated and were not readable because the sun hit them. Who knew? No one ever conveyed that to me. I now had to have more mammograms, right side only. After they were read, I was taken in for an ultrasound.

The radiologist could find no masses in either breast or stated the surgeon I selected was incompetent. She stated she felt it was only a five percent chance I had cancer. To be on the safe side, she stated I should have the biopsy. Because of the location being close to my chest wall, they weren't sure they could even do it.

I left there totally confused. The surgeon I selected was highly recommended. I didn't understand why they were only concerned with my right breast. The imaging facility had stated there was a problem with my left breast as well.

Two days later after work, I set up a meeting with Salisbury Imaging to discuss the discrepancy. They confirmed they had made a mistake. It was indeed the right breast. Now that the information was corrected I could move on with the biopsy that was scheduled for August 24th. Or so I thought. Nope, still more problems. All of my medical records were transferred back to Salisbury Imaging to clear up their error and the hospital where I was to have my biopsy did not have any of my medical records.

I called Salisbury Imaging and they stated my records were sent back to the hospital. August 31st, no one had my medical records. They were lost somewhere. In the meantime, I was set up with a new radiologist from the secretary of administration of the hospital. However, no biopsy could be done until my medical records were located.

On September 8th, I was told they had located my medical records. I was scheduled for the biopsy on September 12th. Three core biopsies were taken. They couldn't tell me anything that day. I had to wait again until they verified the biopsy.

I received a call on September 14th. It was confirmed. I had breast cancer. I dropped the receiver of the phone. I couldn't believe what I was hearing. I felt numb. I knew nothing about breast cancer. What should I do? I remember driving home crying, thinking. *I don't want to die.* I still have so many things I have not accomplished yet in my life. Now I will have to put everything in fast forward. What about my job? What if I end up losing my hair? Cancer, breast cancer, this can't really be happening to me.

The doctor's office set up another appointment for an MRI. They felt it may have spread. On September 27th, I had an appointment with the surgeon to discuss the results of the MRI. When I went, he asked me where my MRI results were. "What?" I said. "Why is that my job?" Another copay and missed time from work for nothing. I was still in limbo and very frustrated, to say the least. I called the hospital. They stated the MRI machine went down halfway through the process, and I would have to come back.

It even gets better. Next, I received a call from the hospital on September 30th. They wanted me to leave work on that same day for blood work and EKG in regard to a pre-op on Monday, October 3rd, because the surgeon scheduled surgery on Tuesday, October 4th.

How can this be? No MRI results. No consultation on what was to take place. I finally threw in the towel and said screw it, enough already. I can't believe I have wasted all this money on copays and lost so much time off work. It's a wonder they didn't fire me. I went back to work so discouraged. My supervisor was anxiously awaiting my arrival by my desk. She asked how it went. I told her that it didn't. That I was done. She told me what I already knew that I couldn't let this go. I told her that whatever happens, happens, that I couldn't continue this frustrating ride. It's a wonder anything gets done correctly in the medical field.

My supervisor left my cubical area, and I began working. I received a call from Stacy in the Human Resource Department. She wanted to talk to me. I immediately thought, *Yup, now I have probably lost my job over all of this nonsense.*

I knocked on her door and she told me to come in. She looked angry. I couldn't read the anger in her face. She told me to sit down and began to explain that my supervisor told her about my dilemma of me wanting to give up on the breast cancer problem. I told her the same. There was no point to keep dealing with this only to get no resolution, only bs from everyone.

She picked up her phone and told me to stay seated. I heard her state she wanted to talk to doctor Tom. They must have said he was with a patient. Then I heard her say, "I need him immediately. Just get him." He must have answered because I heard her explain my situation to him. I overheard her say, "okay," and then she hung up.

She looked at me, straight in the eye, and said, "Tomorrow you will go to this address and meet with Dr. Tom." I reiterated with her that I was done with this situation, but she said with a stern voice, "You need to go", Although hesitant, I was grateful she insisted that I go. I asked her how she knew this doctor and she stated he was a friend of her family.

I arrived at 9:00 am as directed. As soon as I arrived, I noticed several other patients waiting in the waiting room. I wasn't even there five minutes before being directed to go see Dr. Tom. He was young and very caring. He let me know he was sorry about all I had gone through. A welcome change to what I had been dealing with previously. He stated he was not a surgeon but recommended his colleague who was a surgeon to help me figure this all out. Finally, someone who listened!

I was set up with an appointment two days later with Dr. Robinson, a surgeon who had done many breast cancer surgeries.

When Dr. Robinson arrived in the office to meet me, I was taken aback, not only by his kindness but by his thoughtfulness and the time he took explaining what procedure needed to be done. A double mastectomy. I was there in that office for one hour, the longest time any doctor had taken to spend with me since this all transpired.

I went back to work on Monday and thanked Stacy for all her help. What a Godsend she was when I was about to give up entirely.

I had very good insurance at work. It was now time to get everything in place to have surgery. The surgeon recommended a double mastectomy to make sure the cancer was completely gone. From there, I met with an oncologist and a plastic surgeon who would insert the tissue expanders for reconstruction.

I liked all of the doctors, and I felt it was all working out. I had to first pay for my insurance deductible, and then all the doctors requested an upfront amount of money before they would take care of me. All in all, this amounted to several thousands of dollars that I had not anticipated. I was depressed all over again. I had no idea having cancer was such an expensive endeavor.

I was not married to Jimmy, so I did not feel right asking him for the money. I did tell him about everything at which he promised he would do whatever he could.

Back to the Workforce Employment Agency I went. I found several evening cleaning jobs I could pick up for some extra money to cover all the medical expenses. I got a few cleaning jobs, but it was crazy. I would work at the Sawgrass Marriott all day and clean until midnight a couple of nights a week on Beach Boulevard for stores. I thought I was tired before! It was grueling. The surgeon called me wanting to know when I was going to schedule my surgery. I told him I didn't have the money yet. I told him it would be a few more months. He said to make sure it wasn't any longer than that. He said, "I am not going to be responsible if your cancer spreads." Wow, I guess I needed to get that money together soon.

My son Lou was out to sea on a submarine at the time. His wife had been staying in touch with me. She had contacted the Red Cross to get involved. She let me know that if I forwarded them my medical records, my son would be able to get off the sub and meet me and stay while I was hospitalized. On December 9th, 2005, I was scheduled for surgery. My son arrived at Mayport Naval Base in Jacksonville. I picked him up right after work two days prior to my surgery. I was so happy to see him. I was relieved he was going to be able to be with me.

One day before my surgery, Lou and I were out walking. I was showing him a strip mall that I enjoyed walking to often. It was nearing Christmas and there was an ornament display in one of the stores' windows. I happened to see an ornament that resembled my Mom. I said, "Lou, look at that. Looks just like my Mom." He told me to get it. But I told him I was currently trying to hang onto my funds until I got through all of this. We continued walking.

The morning of my surgery, we had to be up early. Lou was up, and Jimmy was starting to get up and planned to take the day off to be with us at the hospital.

It all went as planned. They kept me overnight and part of the following day. The doctor came in and stated all the margins were clear that they had gotten all the cancer. I was thrilled. My son came up early that morning with a gift. I asked him what it was, and he told me to open it. It was the ornament we had seen in the store that resembled my Mom. I was touched. He told me that just as he was about to get it another lady had it in her hand ready to buy it. He explained to her why he wanted it, and she gave it to him. He told her it was the last one the store had in stock, so she let him buy it.

The ornament seemed significant in another way also, but I didn't realize it at the time. The ornament was of a woman dressed in vintage clothing holding a teddy bear. I couldn't believe how much it resembled my Mom for some reason. Years earlier, my son and daughter-in-law had twins. One child Sophia was fine, but they lost her twin sister which they named Faith shortly after giving birth. They always called her teddy bear. I can't help but think the ornament was a way of letting me know that Mom was with the child they had lost.

Lou was a great help, as was Jimmy. I couldn't have been happier having them both there during that time. A couple of weeks later, it was time for Lou to return home to be with his family for Christmas. I was so grateful for our time together.

I was finally released to go back to work. I planned to have reconstruction later on, so that meant I needed more time off once the tissue expanders were complete, which took a while. The second surgery was a lot easier, and downtime was not as long.

I took away so much from this experience. When you're diagnosed with a serious illness, you have to be your own advocate. Don't let the doctors make all your decisions. You have to take on the role of researching the disease. What avenue works for one individual may not work for the next. I went to the library only to find outdated material from years ago. They had photos of women who had reconstruction that looked horrible. I knew this avenue wasn't for me. I needed to do more research from a different source.

I then contacted the American Cancer Society. They mailed brochures to me with the most current information on procedures and techniques.

I would definitely recommend contacting them for cancer information. Once you have made a decision, find capable doctors. I went to many different doctors before making up my mind about which one to go to, and it was well worth it. My reconstructive surgery looks nothing like those ugly pictures that were at the library. However, the healing process takes a lot of time, which I had not planned on. You have to be patient knowing the outcome will be worth it.

After all was said and done, I was given three to five years to live. I was told to take the prescription Tamoxifen for five years, if I made it that long. I am not a doctor, but again I did my own research on Tamoxifen. After researching all I could find out about the drug, I decided the drug had too many side effects. I was not okay with it, so I declined to take anything.

As time passed, every time I felt ill, I would wonder if the cancer had returned. I didn't want to run to the doctor every time I felt sick, but it remained in the back of my mind that maybe the cancer had returned. Then when I did go to the doctor for a checkup, the cancer was always in remission. I decided that this was crazy. Why was I letting myself worry about the 'what ifs?' I needed to get on with living or get on with dying. I learned that it's a little hard to do both at the same time.

I decided to get on with living and not look back. Currently, I am better. I feel good, and life is now back to normal. I received a call from the doctor's office years later wanting to know how I was. I told them that I was great and thanked them for checking. The next thing they wanted to know was if there were any significant side effects from the Tamoxifen. I then let them know that I never took it. They put the doctor on the phone right away. He said, sternly, that I was supposed to take that to keep the cancer from returning. I said, "Well, I am still here with no cancer years after your prediction, so I guess I didn't need Tamoxifen after all." What could he say after that? He finally told me that he was glad I was doing well and quickly hung up before I could respond.

I believe my decision to not spend any more time worrying about cancer has been significant to my living-on all these additional years. I do not believe any doctor should tell a patient how long they have to live. It just adds to a negative mindset. They should say you're going to live as long as you are supposed to live. We are all going to die sometime at some point, but I don't think it's the doctor's call to make.

*The Negative: It was a long, annoying process, finally accomplishing surgery and the time it took to recover and heal. I was given three to five years to live.

*The Positive: I survived the ordeal and am still here seventeen years later with no relapses of cancer. It was like childbirth, painful, but then you forget about that part of the experience and enjoy what lies ahead.

Chapter 10

Panama City? Really?

While I was still recuperating on the couch one evening, Jimmy came home all smiles. A close friend of his offered him a job in Panama City. He would be making a much better income. I told him he should go. He wanted me to go also, but I still was off work on sick leave, and it was a lot to take in along with everything else that was going on with me.

He moved to Panama City while I stayed behind in Jacksonville. When I was able to drive again, he asked me to join him. The trip to Panama City from Jacksonville is roughly a five-hour drive. I decided to head over and visit before I had to return to work. My initial thought of Panama City was, *Na, I don't think I want to live there*. He continued to convince me to go back, I sent out some resumes, but my heart was in Jacksonville.

I couldn't decide whether to move to Panama City and be with Jimmy or to stay in

Jacksonville by myself. It was hard to leave the place I had come to love, Jacksonville, but I did go and got a job in Panama City not long after moving there.

Although Jimmy and I were great friends and always got along well, our relationship began deteriorating as time passed. As an asbestos project manager, he was spending a lot of hours buried with work or being on the phone constantly setting up plans. I would come home from work, and he barely noticed I was even in the house. It was nearing December, and the company he worked for was planning a Christmas party in Gainesville, and he asked me to join him. The company was providing overnight stays at a hotel after the party. I thought maybe this could be a positive way to get some time with him as it would be a four-hour drive from Panama City and maybe have a chance for us to catch up and get closer again.

I had not finished all of the surgeries in regard to my breast cancer. I had no nipples, and yet I was grateful I was okay and healthy, but I still felt less of a woman without them. Jimmy had offered to buy me a new dress for the Christmas party. I was so excited. I went down to the mall and found a beautiful dress in Macy's. I couldn't wait to go home and show it to Jimmy. He thought it looked great on me. I couldn't have been happier. Things were looking good for our holiday getaway.

As we were getting ready to leave for the weekend that evening, a co-worker of his called and wanted to know if he and his wife could ride along with us. *Great,* I thought. *I was hoping to have this time alone with Jimmy so we could discuss personal things about us.*

Although they joined us, it was a pleasant trip. When we arrived, we checked into our room and then proceeded to the ballroom. It looked absolutely beautiful. At that moment I was so excited, I knew we were going to have a great evening. We joined some of his other co-workers at the table. They had a live band, and we had a great time dancing. When it was over, we went back to our room. I was looking forward to some quiet romantic time. Jimmy left to get some ice but didn't return right away. I found him in the hallway talking to a girl from his firm. *No big deal,* I thought, *he will be back momentarily.* I decided to take a shower and freshen up. The hotel allowed smoking in the ballroom, and since I did not smoke, I wanted to get rid of the cigarette smell from my hair and clothes.

An hour had passed, and Jimmy was still not back. Then two hours, three hours. I couldn't sleep. I went looking for him and asked other co-workers I ran into if they had seen him, but no one knew where he was. Wow, it seemed like DeJa'Vu all over again, as with my first ex-husband. I went back to our room and tried to sleep, but I couldn't. The more I thought about it, the angrier I got. Was it the breast cancer, or was it my feelings that were haunting me, that he was just with me to have someone around. I knew we were good friends not planning on marriage, but I thought even good friends don't pull this shit. It was now 6 am. I walked out to the truck they had given him to use. I had the key in my hand. I thought, *Hell I could just leave them all here and go home.* But since it was not his truck, but a company truck, I thought the company would say I had stolen it. As I was sitting there, he came over and asked, "Why are you out here?"

"Really, where have you been all night?" He had no answer. Now I **know** the answer. We checked out and it was the quietest ride home ever. I couldn't scream or say anything because of our other riders. But I really wanted to have a serious discussion with him right away. When we arrived home, I insisted we talk, but he wanted no part of it. I decided I was not going to put myself through the bullshit of being taken advantage of once again.

I found a nice apartment not far from work. Jimmy seemed blindsided when I was packing. I told him if he really wanted me, he wouldn't play games. After all I had been through, I didn't deserve this. The marriage idea didn't matter. If I was to be with someone there needed to be respect, and that respect needed to go both ways.

*The Negative: I was blindsided once again by someone I thought was a true friend.

*The Positive: I needed time to reevaluate my relationships with men. I now had the time and a new place to do that.

Chapter 11

Unexpected Voice From Beyond

I was lying on the couch one morning, just relaxing, enjoying the quiet. I didn't want to watch television. All of a sudden, I heard a voice almost like someone was there, but there was no one there but me. I couldn't help but think they must have given me some good drugs during my surgery. The voice requested for me to call my sister. Now I am starting to freak out. "What", I said to the air in the room. "Who is this? Who is talking to me?"

"It's your Mother," came the reply from thin air.

"Sure," I said. "I went through all of the psychic development classes and never heard anything from you. Why now?" I inquired. I decided to continue with the conversation. She asked me to call my sister. "What sister?" I said.

"Your older sister," came the reply.

I have not stayed in touch that much with any of my family members since moving to Florida. I think the last time I had spoken to my older sister was five months prior. I asked the voice why she insisted I call my sister. The voice told me my sister was having marital problems. Her husband took up with another woman who rides motorcycles, and I could help her get through it.

A little background on my sister. I introduced her to her husband back in high school, and they have been together for over thirty-two years. They take motorcycle trips. They each have their own bike and go riding in groups. I always thought that was cool. I was very skeptical about the voice I was hearing and decided not to call my sister.

I didn't mention this to anyone because I thought they would think I was losing it. Still, curiosity was getting to me after about a week. I thought, *Awe, what the hell. I will call her.*

The phone rang twice, and her husband answered. I said hello and asked him how he was doing, but he didn't answer. I asked him if I could talk to my sister. He informed me that she didn't live there anymore. *WHAT? Where is she?* He then proceeded to give me her new telephone number, and we ended the call. I could surmise he didn't want to talk to me. I was in shock. Now I began to wonder if it was Mom and not just some voice I was hearing from the drugs I was given at the hospital, I bit the bullet and made the call to my sister at her new number. Her first words to me were to ask me how I got her new number. I told her I had called her house and her husband gave it to me. I said, "What's going on?"

She stated exactly what I was already told by the voice. Her husband had taken up with another woman biker they both knew, and my sister left him. I told her I already knew, and she wanted to know how I knew. I was convinced it really was Mom telling me about it, and I told my sister that our Mom told me. The phone went silent for several moments. I finally asked if she was still there, and she said yes, but what I had told her was crazy. I told her that I knew how it sounded. No one else had called me to tell me this information. I had no idea. As strange as it sounds, it was bittersweet. I was happy to finally have communication with my Mom but was very sad about my sister's situation.

I decided to keep in touch with my sister on a more regular basis although I really wasn't sure how Mom thought I could help her. I would call my sister and listen to all her painful conversations about how this all transpired with her husband. I knew she loved him despite what had happened, and I know he loved her. I told her that sometimes there is miscommunication in a marriage, as was with my husband and myself. I truly think if we sat down and talked about what was missing in the marriage, it may have had a different outcome. I urged her to go talk to her husband. She stated the new girl had already moved into their home. I told her to go anyway, and she did. It took time, but they started spending more time together, and the new girl moved out.

My sister demanded they update everything, new bed, new furniture, everything. She just could not accept another woman on her furniture. Her husband agreed.

My sister and her husband came to visit me in Panama City a few months after they had gotten back together. They came during Bike Week, no less. Bike week in Panama City is like a free-for-all. I was concerned with the hotel where they had chosen to stay. I was going to get them a room a little outside of the chaos, but they wanted to be in the middle of it all. The hotel they stayed at had a Tiki bar and had a band. They asked me to come to listen to the band one night. I felt in my heart it could be DeJa'Vu all over again for them, but I went despite what I thought might happen.

As I was walking into the Tiki bar at their hotel, I noticed several women with no blouses on, no bra tops, nothing, naked from the waist up. *Oh boy,* I thought, *this is like adding fuel to the fire.* I joined my sister and her husband at a table where they were sitting and having a cocktail. The waitress came over to take my drink order with no blouse on, *yikes,* I thought. I watched my brother-in-law's eyes. He never once stared at her breasts. Wow, I was shocked because every other guy there was enjoying the many views. My sister got up to go to the ladies' room. I walked off not far from our table, keeping a close eye wanting to see if my brother-in-law was going to act differently with both of us not there at the table with him, but he did not. I was so proud of him.

It was at that moment that I realized they would be fine. He took my sister to every place she wanted to go on their visit. When they left I knew all would be good with them and their marriage. I guess Mom felt I could be of some type of assistance in getting their marriage back on track. But I feel it was them and not really me having a lot to do with it.

*The Negative: I couldn't believe after thirty-two years of marriage, two individuals so connected as my sister and my brother-in-law would choose to separate.

*The Positive: I was so proud they spent the time to reunite and create a stronger bond in their marriage. I learned if two people care enough for each other, it's inevitable they will be together.

Chapter 12

New Place, Different Mindset

I was totally enjoying my new apartment. My apartment was on the third floor. Most tenants do not want to be three floors up due to having to climb up the stairs. The complex had no elevator, but I didn't mind. I thought it would be great exercise to climb the stairs every day. It was good, except for on moving day, when I had to go up and down the stairs so often. It was a bit overwhelming, but I got through it. I didn't have to move furniture because I had to purchase that as I never owned any in Panama City while living with Jimmy. A short time later the furniture was all delivered, and I was truly enjoying my alone time.

On weekends, I started spending a lot of time at the downtown marina. The sunsets were magnificent. Sitting in solitude watching the sunset made it a great place to reflect on my life and figure out where I wanted my life direction to go from here.

I would watch the boats come into the dock. I enjoyed watching the sailboats even more. They looked so peaceful catching the wind and heeling on their side while sailing. The more I observed them, the more I was drawn to them. I thought about how cool it would be to be out on the ocean letting your sails glide you across the water to wherever the wind blew.

One evening while sitting on the dock, a gentleman who was on a sailboat got off and came over and introduced himself as Jack. He asked me if I had a sailboat there at the marina. I told him that I didn't, but I wished I did. He reiterated how great it is to sail. He asked if I had ever been out sailing, and I told him that I hadn't. He asked me if I would like to learn. I told him that I would love to learn how to sail. He talked about all of his sailing adventures and of how he had purchased his forty-foot wooden ketch sailboat from the east coast of Florida and sailed it up to Panama City. He lived on his sailboat. He offered to show it to me, but I declined as I didn't know this guy from Adam. He said he was alone and for me to come down anytime, and he understood why I was unsure of him just meeting him for the first time

The following weekend I returned to the dock at the city marina and ran into Jack again. He would explain more information about sailing and the logistics of it all. I found myself very interested not only in Jack but also in sailing and his knowledge of it. Jack was retired, enjoying life to its fullest. He could come and go whenever he wanted. No limits. The ocean could take him anywhere he chose to go.

We continued to communicate and had lunch on the dock on weekends. I would make sandwiches at my apartment and bring them for us to eat on the dock next to where his sailboat was docked. We talked more about his sailing adventures. As time passed, I felt more comfortable with him, and he let me onto his sailboat. He kept it in immaculate condition. He also had a cat he had adopted that had been a stray at the marina. The cat was quite skittish, as was I.

I ended up spending almost every weekend down on Jack's sailboat. I was so intrigued by the peacefulness of it all. Up to that point, we had never gone out sailing. I was just taking in all of the information he had to share with me. He had a Captain's license he showed me one time. He was originally from Illinois. He went to college and studied Mortuary Science to be in the family funeral business, but he wanted no part of it after college. He just wanted to be free of that situation. After receiving his Captain's license he captained a tour boat out of Fort Lauderdale before coming to Panama City. Once in Panama City, he took out local navy divers from the local Navy Base near Thomas Drive in Panama City Beach before retiring.

One night, he confided in me that he had been on medication due to being depressed. I assumed he was fine at that point because he acted very normal to me during all of the times we were together.

One evening he asked me if I was serious about sailing and would I like to go out with him on a short-run to get the feel of sailing sometime soon. The short run would be to Shell Island which was not that far away. I was thrilled. We were planning on leaving early the next Saturday morning. The weather cooperated, and it was going to be a beautiful day. We left early around seven am. The sun was just coming up. Once we were under sail, his cell phone rang. I didn't pay a whole lot of attention to him talking on the phone as I was steering the helm, feeling great.

I wanted to know and learn everything there was to learn about sailing. It intrigued me. Every half hour his phone continued to ring, and he answered it every time. I asked him if everything was okay. He assured me everything was fine. But then he confided in me that he had a female friend whom he went to college with that stayed in close touch with him, and she was calling him to make sure everything was okay. I asked him if it was a problem with me sailing with him and he stated it wasn't. I guess I was so wrapped up in learning about sailing that I didn't really care about all of the phone calls. Once we hit international waters, he took the helm, and I began to not feel so good. I was getting seasick. He said to look ahead at land, but it really didn't help. He said we'd head back, but first we'd anchor for a while. Perfect I thought. The bouncing of the water just continued to make me feel sick. I told him I was going to jump off and go for a swim. Once I did that I felt a whole lot better. He also jumped in, and we chatted as we swam. Other boats were going by, but slowed down when they saw us in the water. He said he would help me learn all there was to know about sailing. I thought, *what a nice guy.* I felt a connection with him, not in a physical way but in a friendship way. We got back on the sailboat, and we had the lunch I had prepared prior.

As we headed back towards the marina, the wind had dyed off, so we were motoring in when the motor stopped. Jack spent about an hour working on it and was able to get it running enough to get us back to his dock. I didn't realize all the complications there were to sail. I just knew sailing was my newfound love.

Jack and I continued to pursue sailing dates together. Whenever we were together his cell phone would continue to go off. It was the same girl. I asked him if there was more to the story than he was admitting, but he would always say that there wasn't, that they were just friends. *Okay*, I thought. *Then I am not going to worry about it,* and I didn't. We would continue sailing, and I was learning something new every time. The last time we went out on the sailboat, I was watching the depth finder. There was a sandbar we needed to keep an eye out for so we wouldn't get stuck. The keel was five feet and would make us go aground if we sailed into it. Unfortunately, It came up fast, and we stopped. Jack knew exactly what had happened and jumped out and tried to move the boat, but it was too far aground. He radioed for help, and we were quickly towed off the sandbar. We were soon back on course. By then, it was getting late, so we just headed back to the marina.

As time progressed, Jack and I had become wonderful friends. I never wanted anything else but to be friends with him. He took me to a concert in Tallahassee one evening, and we had a great time. His other female friend seemed to dislike me from the information I had gotten from the other liveaboard community he belonged to, but I didn't let that get in my way. I figured if he liked her that much, he would be with her. His birthday came around, and I got him a cake and a card. But he said his other female friend was coming by, and it would be uncomfortable for both of us to be there, so I just left. I didn't think a lot of it. I decided to distance myself from the situation as I didn't want to cause problems. After all, it wasn't so much about him as it was about his knowledge and the experiences I was taking in from sailing with him.

One day while at work, I received a text message from Jack saying that he missed me. And that he had just located the birthday card I had left for him, and he was so sad. Not giving it much thought, I told him not to worry about it. I told him I would touch base with him after I was off work. He wrote back and said, 'You can't toss love." I had no idea what he was talking about at that point. I was never in love, nor did I feel he was, but again said I would talk to him about it later.

When I got off work, I called him, but he didn't answer his phone. It was the other girl, the one he had spoken about that he went to college with, who answered the phone. I told her I was returning a call to Jack, and she stated he would not be answering since he is dead. WHAT? I just texted with him earlier today. I thought it was some sick joke she was playing on me. I said, "What are you talking about?" She told me that he went to a nearby park this afternoon, put a gun to his head, and killed himself. I was shocked. How could this have happened? I never saw the signs. She completely blamed me for his death. I couldn't believe it. I kept backtracking my steps, thinking of what I could have done differently, or why he got the impression of being in love. We never stated that to each other. It was a very bazaar situation.

*The Negative: I lost a good friend whom I had no idea would commit suicide. I never saw the signs. I was emotionally drained after that situation and did blame myself for not seeing it coming.

*The Positive: I will never take it lightly when someone tells me they have depression. I will pay closer attention to the signs. I am grateful we had time together and that he took an interest in teaching me the fundamentals of sailing. I will never forget his kindness.

Chapter 13

My Desire To Sail Continued

Moving on after Jack's death was difficult for me. I couldn't stop thinking about how I was so driven to sail and to be out on the water and all of the knowledge Jack had and shared with me. I felt a strong connection to purchase a sailboat of my own after our short encounters out on the water. There was something about being at peace out on the water. Sailing was different than going out on a motorboat. Once you're out on the water, the wind takes you, and when the wind changes, you have to adjust the sails to the situation, kind of like life. It was something I really enjoyed doing. After much thought, I decided to purchase a sailboat and live the dream instead of dreaming the dream. I wasn't sure how I would be able to afford it though, living in an apartment and having a new car payment and of my other expenses. I took and passed an American Sailing Association 101 course and started looking online for a small boat, but I had to decide first what kind of boat I wanted.

I wanted a boat that was bigger than a pocket sailboat but smaller than a forty-footer. I was thinking along the lines of a twenty-five to a thirty-foot vessel. I would go online whenever I had time and scope them out. I sometimes would spend hours looking for a sailboat. It was kind of bizarre how the thought of having a boat of my own intrigued me.

In researching, I found the Hunter, Catalina, and O'Days were great starter boats. They all had their pros and cons. The Catalina was a good boat for the money, but the sailing performance was listed as average. The O'Day was a good boat but was listed as having deck core problems. The Hunter's only con I read was it was not recommended for crossing the ocean. It was more a boat for short runs, and that was exactly what I wanted in a sailboat.

Three months later, while searching ads on craigslist, I saw an older Hunter twenty-five-foot sailboat for sale at a marina near me. Thankfully this was not the marina where Jack's sailboat had been. A different marina. The photos looked great, and it also had a new Honda four-stroke motor. The seller wasn't asking much for the boat as he was anxious to sell it because he was moving and couldn't take it with him. I called him and asked if I could see it. He stated others were wanting to see it also and were going to stop by that day. We scheduled a time for me to go and take a look. When I arrived at the small marina, I was impressed with the sailboat but not necessarily where it was docked. It was a dive, a sketchy kind of place. Needless to say, I did like the boat. It had good sails, a Danforth anchor, an almost new marine radio, and a great Honda motor. Everything looked good to me. I was inexperienced at this whole buying a used sailboat situation. I just knew I wanted to do it. I told the seller that I would think about it and get back to him. I told him that I didn't like where the boat was docked. He let me know I could always move it after I bought it or keep it there. I went back to my apartment but couldn't stop thinking about the boat. I wanted it, but how could I make it happen? Then a lightbulb went off. Why couldn't I give up my apartment and be a liveaboard instead?

I called the bank on Monday to see if I could get a loan. The banker stated they would give me the loan based on the condition that I give up the apartment and live aboard the sailboat. I could get the loan as long as it didn't cost more for me to live on the boat than it did for me to live in the apartment. (Mistake #1) Hindsight is twenty-twenty it is said, and in my experience, it is true. One should never purchase things based on emotions, but that is just what I did.

I was thrilled. I called the seller back, and thankfully he hadn't sold the boat yet. The bank insisted on taking photos, and surveying the boat to verify it was worthy of them to give me the loan. The bank called me a week later and stated it was approved. I sealed the deal. I was so happy, but next came another problem. I wanted to move the boat to a different marina. There were several in the Panama City area. Everyone I called was booked well into the following year as far as liveaboard availability. (Mistake #2) I thought there had to be some other place, but there wasn't. I decided I would put my name in at all the liveaboard marina places as they told me sometimes folks change their mind, and it could happen sooner. I thought I'd have to bite the bullet and live at the sketchy marina for now.

I had to get a storage unit to unload my belongings from my apartment first, and then I canceled my lease. Even though I was entering unknown territory, I was still excited.

The first day I pulled up into the marina, I was met by a thin man named John. He lived in an apartment right on the water with a fence around it. Inside the fence was a large pit bull dog who barked and growled and wanted to tear down the fence to get at me. John told me not to worry about the dog that he barked at everyone. His name was Blue. *Who names their dog Blue*, I thought. But nothing was a surprise at this place. John offered to help if needed. He informed me that he looked out for the folks on the boats. It was like entering a whole other world I'd never seen before. I went from living in a beautiful apartment to living in a disarranged marina. While driving into the marina, one couldn't miss seeing old unkempt mobile homes, some were half-painted one color and half-painted another color. There were a lot of old cars sitting out front with missing parts. It looked like a junkyard. This marina was not a place I felt all warm and fuzzy about and cringed when I thought about having to live there.

Although I despised the place, it was home now. I found it interesting as time went on, and I got to know some of the folks that lived there.

I moved a few things onto the boat. Most importantly, I had to have my coffee pot and my hot plate to make dinners. I arranged things on the boat and did some painting to make it more like home. The marina had a nice bathroom facility with showers that could lock while you were in there, so I felt safe. The bathroom was the only decent thing about the marina and for sure a necessity as I didn't have a shower on the boat.

The first night sleeping on the boat was fabulous. I slept like a baby. I never realized the rocking could be so relaxing.

There was another liveaboard at this marina named Bob, who lived three boats away. He was always yelling and starting fights with people. I was warned by others who lived there that he was a Vietnam vet and to stay clear of him. *Great*, I thought, *what did I get myself into here?*

One Saturday morning, I woke up to someone knocking on my boat. It was none other than Barnacle Bob, as he was known. We referred to him that way because he had so many barnacles on his boat, and he never cleaned them off. I couldn't imagine what he could possibly want with me. I was going to pretend I wasn't there, but it was pretty obvious with my car sitting a short distance away that I was home. I very slowly opened my hatch. There stood Bob holding a rolled-up chart in his hand. He told me he knew that I was new here and to sailing, and he had an extra chart of the area, so I'd know the depth and where I was going in this area.

I was shocked. I didn't know what to say. Bob was very nice, and I thought that was kind of him to give me that map. After that happened, I wasn't taken back by him anymore.

I also spent more time with John on the dock. He liked to fish and would bring his pit bull, who ended up being a great dog by the way, not so good first impression though. After he caught some fish, he would grill them and share them with all the other liveaboards. I was starting to realize this was not as bad of a place as I had initially thought.

One Fourth of July, we rounded up several people onto my boat and motored down toward the city marina for the fireworks. After the fireworks, we tried sailing back, but there was no wind. We had to motor back, but I enjoyed it anyway. I didn't sail often because I was actually enjoying just living on my new boat.

One weekend morning, when I was going off to the store, John asked me where I was going. I told him I was going to the store. He asked if I would go up to the gas station and get him some live shrimp to fish with along with a bait bucket to put them in so he could keep the catch fresh. I told him

I would, and he handed me the money to pay for everything. He wanted a dozen live bait shrimp.

When I got to the store, there were several bait buckets in all different colors, including a hot pink one. Of course, I had to get that one for John, just to be a smart ass. When I got to the counter, the guy told me to pay for the shrimp and then go out and get them. "Ah, no," I said. "I am not going to get the shrimp myself. Can you get them for me?" He did, and now all I had to do was drive them back, give them to John, and then do my shopping.

I put the bait bucket on the passenger side floor and proceeded to drive back to the marina. Just as I was pulling in, a car pulled out in front of me, and I had to stop quickly. The whole hot pink bait bucket of shrimp tipped over, water and shrimp were everywhere. My new car reeked of fish smell. I got all the shrimp back in the bucket, so much for not wanting to touch them. I took them to John and gave him back the change. He was so excited he told me that he couldn't believe the guy gave me two dozen live shrimp and only changed for one dozen. From now on, he said he would be sending me up there for the shrimp. I let him know I'd never do that again and told him about the bucket spilling and shrimp crawling all around inside my car. I had to take out the carpeted mats and lay them on the dock until I could get back to clean them properly later.

A few months later, an opening for a dock space had come available at the downtown marina. Finally, my boat could be docked at a modern facility with a dock locker and nicer showers. My boat now sat between two beautiful, larger sailboats. I loved it. It wasn't long before meeting all the other owners that had boats docked there. One couple, in particular, Joe Bob and Tami (aka LT), owned a beautiful sailboat farther down the dock. I found them interesting and intriguing. At first, I didn't know what to think of them. Joe Bob would ask me to go out for dinner when Tami would be visiting her family. I always declined, and he would tell me if I needed any help with boat repairs to let him know.

The situation felt awkward. I chatted with both Joe Bob and Tami as often as I felt comfortable. It always seemed like when she wasn't there, Bob would invite me to whatever was happening around town. Maybe he felt sorry for me being alone, or maybe he was just trying to be a friend. I wasn't sure right off the bat, but I soon came to a different conclusion. I told him I would go out only if Tami would go along as well. One night we decided the three of us would go out to Chili's for dinner.

True to form, Joe Bob drove an old Chevy Van. It only had two front seats and no other back seats except for a lawn chair. I told them I would sit in the back in the lawn chair. Tami insisted I ride up front. Okay, I did as she suggested. On the ride, I couldn't help but wonder how these two unique individuals met. So at the restaurant, while waiting for our food, I asked Tami about it. She told me that it was a funny story. Tami worked at a dental office and had stopped at a gas station on the way to work for coffee and gas. Before getting the gas, she went in to get the coffee but couldn't reach the cups (where the initials LT came from, Little Tami). Joe Bob happened to be standing there, so Tami asked him to get her a cup. As she was fixing her coffee, Joe Bob was talking to her, wanting her to go out with him. Tami wanted no part of it and told him so. She paid for the coffee and gas and went out to pump the gas. Joe Bob took this opportunity to ask the gas station attendant not to turn Tami's pump on just yet. Joe Bob then proceeded to go out and talk to her some more to try to convince her to go out with him. In the meantime, Tami was on the speaker, by the gas pump, asking the attendant why the pump wasn't working. When Joe Bob interrupted her and continued on his quest to get her to go out, he stated he had asked the attendant to hold her gas pump up so he could try to convince her to go out. Finally, he told her that she would be missing out on a great opportunity and that she needed to act fast because he might be off the market soon. She couldn't help but laugh and gave in to him. They have been together ever since.

Joe Bob and Tami ended up being very helpful to me with regards to my boat and warning me of situations on the dock. People I should be careful around and things like that. I continued to enjoy their company. One evening, in particular, I had planned to go out with a guy who frequented the dock area. It was just a casual dinner, not a date exactly, as I told him I wasn't interested in any commitments at that time. Joe Bob told me he didn't like him and to think about maybe not going. I didn't think much of it. I was only going to dinner, and it was going to be a public place. No big deal, or so I thought.

The entire evening, the guy was so jealous every time I casually looked at a guy or said something about another guy. He would go on and on about it. Finally, I just asked him to take me back home, and thankfully he did. He was so angry. Just as we pulled into the parking spot in front of my boat, we got out of the car as Joe Bob pulled up in his Chevy Van. Joe Bob rolled his window down and said, "Hey Girlfriend, if looks could kill." It was so funny. Joe Bob told me later he did that on purpose. It felt like he was my big brother looking out for me. I thanked him for doing that.

Even though my sailboat was much smaller than the others docked at that marina, I was glad I had experienced owning a sailboat. Although I had no idea the upkeep on a boat would be so expensive, I still enjoyed the experience. For one thing, the boat has to be hauled out of the water every so often for the bottom to be repainted, because the seawater and barnacles take their toll. You also have to have it moved if bad weather threatens. The marina makes that call for all of the boat owners at the marina. If the boat owner doesn't move their boat once the marina has made the call in bad weather, they move it for you and bill you later. You then have to have an alternative place to live when this happens if you are living aboard.

Some people with boats at the dock have had their mast hit by lightning or lost all their electrical components, damage like that. It never happened to me, though. Owning a boat turned out to be a lot more work and expense than I had anticipated. On a positive note, I have never slept better in my life. The rocking of the boat was comforting and very relaxing. I continued to go to work even though getting ready in the morning was a bit more of a challenge with less room to get ready and the boat constantly moving. But having coffee sitting out on the stern as the sun was coming up each morning was priceless.

The woman who was the receptionist where I worked was single, and so was I. Her name was Jean. She thought it was great I was living on a boat. We became great friends. She was a jack of all trades. I felt so beneath her, and yet she thought I had it all going on. We spent time together outside of work. I told her I was going to Hawaii for Christmas. It was my second time visiting the Island of Oahu. Arriving in Honolulu is like entering an Island of paradise, the beaches are amazing. My son and his family were stationed in Pearl Harbor at the time. My Dad had also been stationed at the same base when he was in the Army. So it really had a special meaning to me. I was so excited. I was planning on staying for ten days. The only downfall was the flight was leaving at 4:00 in the morning, which meant I had to get up super early. I told her that I hoped I wouldn't miss the flight. I told her that I was planning on leaving my car at the airport for 10 days. She told me that was crazy. She suggested that she should pick me up in the morning and drive me to the airport. That way I wouldn't have to pay so much for the parking. I told her there was no way I would ever expect anyone to get up that early, drive me to the airport, and then have to go to work all day.

While getting ready for my trip that morning, thanking God I didn't oversleep, my phone started ringing. It was Jean. She was already here to take me to the airport. *WHAT?* She even had coffee and breakfast for me, too. I couldn't believe it, what a great friend.

During the next few months, we spent a lot of time together just enjoying dinners out or at each other's homes. She talked about wanting to move to Clearwater to do interior decorating. I admitted to her my desire to move to Bradenton as they had a great marina there to keep my boat and still live aboard. We would spend hours talking about how we would accomplish our different goals. She owned a home and had a lot of possessions where I didn't. Every time we talked about our moves, her eyes would light up. I knew she would be happier doing what she really desired. But then, one day, when I chatted with her at work about it, she seemed to lose the drive she had. I asked her if she changed her mind, and she said she hadn't. It's just that she was too old and would start to tear up. *WHAT?* I told her she wasn't dead, and neither was I. I told her it was time for us to just do it. With her being in Clearwater, which is not all that far from Bradenton, we could still get together. She even admitted to me that one weekend she had driven there and looked for a place to live.

I told her not to give up on her dream, and then I knew she would be happy. A few weeks later, I noticed she was taking a lot of time off work. She told me she was seeing a doctor and wasn't feeling all that well. The following day she came into work, and both of her eyes were bloodshot. I asked if she had been crying, but she said she just had a terrible headache. I told her to go home or back to the doctor, but she refused because she had taken time off from work the prior week. She called me from the hospital that same evening. She ended up in the hospital because her blood pressure was extremely high. I visited her once she was back home, and she assured me they had told her she would be fine. I was feeling better for her knowing they gave her the okay to leave the hospital and recuperate at home. They told her not to go back to work for a couple of days, so I stopped by to visit her again one day after work. She seemed different. She asked me to light some candles she had out on her lanai. I didn't know why she wanted me to do that, but I did it. Almost as soon as I lit them, she told me to blow them out. She wanted to lie down. I hugged her, and then I left. That was the last time I saw her. She died the next day of a brain aneurysm.

I learned the news from my supervisor at work that my friend had passed. I was devastated. I lost such a great friend. I was not only sad that Jean had passed, but I was also sad she never made it to Clearwater to fulfill her dream. They hadn't hired a replacement for her, so I was asked to fill in and sit in her chair. I hated it. Even her picture of her dog just sat there on her desk staring at me. It was a very emotional time for me, of course. Every time I had to sit in her chair, it took a toll on me. I felt so stuck in my situation.

Not long after, I decided to take the plunge and move to Bradenton. On weekends I did what my friend Jean had done. I went to Bradenton to look for a place to live. I changed my mind about living on the boat after trying to find a way to get it there, and the price of the liveaboard was much more expensive than where I had it in Panama City. I found an apartment in Bradenton and left my job after working there for nine years. I tried diligently to sell the boat, and after getting no buyers, I called the bank. I took a loss on it, and they took it back. I needed to move on, and letting the boat go took one more weight off my shoulders.

Since moving, I have gotten employment and am living in Bradenton and certainly not enjoying apartment life. I was awakened many nights by the tenants below me arguing loudly late at night. I had just gotten a job and did not appreciate being woken up by a policeman knocking on my door at two in the morning, wanting to know what took place downstairs from me. I complained many times, and they just blew me off. I started looking for alternative places to live. Low and behold, I found an RV resort with lots to rent at a reasonable rate. Now all I had to do was find a travel trailer to put on it. It wasn't long before I found one, paid cash for it, and the rest is pretty much history. I broke my lease and moved into a fifth-wheel travel trailer. It was one of the best decisions I have ever made.

*The Negative: I lost a very close friend and coworker suddenly. Another death of a friend and I hadn't done sufficient homework about the upkeep and the expenses including maintenance of the motor, insurance, additional sea tow coverage (if you should break down while out on the water.), and slip fee involved was a big mistake. Living aboard a boat is challenging if you are doing it alone. Anything can happen that you may not be prepared to handle.

*The Positive: I missed Jean, but I have a lot of great memories of the fun times we had together, and If I hadn't gotten the boat, I would have always wondered what it would be like to have one. Sometimes even if it doesn't work out, you can cross it off your bucket list that you did it. I also made some great friends I continue to stay in touch with even though I no longer have the boat.

Chapter 14

Moving on from Life's Challenges

I realized the issues that were holding me back and not catapulting me forward.

* MENTAL ANGUISH = POOR CHOICES

The two go hand in hand. It's hard for me to admit this was the majority of my life. No, I never went to a psychiatrist for help. I trusted God to get me where I needed to be eventually. He certainly was not on my time frame most of the time, though. I believe that was because God wanted me to stay in the situation until I finished learning something that I needed to take away from the experience, and then I could move on to a better place. I continued to pray and vent.

Through these experiences, I have had and made the previous choices throughout my life. I have made some I would never repeat. Life is full of learning curves, but if you don't fall on your face, you may think the bad choices you are making are acceptable.

When you're a child at the age of five, and someone asks you what you want to be when you grow up, you don't say you want to be homeless. If you are homeless something happened to trigger you to be homeless.

When my husband left I rolled pennies to get gas and go to work praying I'd make it before I ran out of gas. I never did run out of gas even when the gas gauge showed empty. I refused to ask family and friends for help even though I know I should have. I wanted to fix the problem myself. I was so devastated at the time, hence that was a bad decision not to ask for help.

*YOU NEED VALUABLE PEOPLE IN YOUR LIFE

Over the years, I have learned the value of the significance of having people in your life. Almost everyone has many friends. I have gone on Facebook, and some of my friends have over one thousand friends. Wow, that's great, but I am talking here about friends that would drop anything to help you out. These are the ones you need most.

I always wanted to write a book to inspire others positively through my crazy experiences in life. If it weren't for a good friend, it probably wouldn't have ever happened. I met her by fate one day while at a pool. We stayed in touch, and she reached out to me one day and asked me if I was ever going to write that book. I wanted to write it, but life kept getting in the way. I would send her a page here and there, and when she didn't hear from me, she would always ask if I had any more pages. She is a Godsend to me because even though I wanted to do this, I might not have finished it if she hadn't insisted I continue. She is my cheerleader and believes in me. We all need that in life.

My unique handful of friends were Marie, my friend since 4th grade, my daughter-in-law, Dani, Stacy, my human resource friend, Judy, my co-worker friend, and previously Jean, who had passed away.

I no longer try to resolve problems on my own without praying and contacting my close friends for input if I had a tough decision to make. It is not one-sided, since they know they can count on me also. Close relationships are key to making better choices in life. Even if you don't agree with them, it will give you a different perspective to think about.

Family for me is kind of bittersweet. As an in-law in my first marriage, it was delightful. I loved my mother-in-law and all my husband's siblings. I continue to stay in touch with them from time to time.

My Mom and Dad were great when they were alive. However, my siblings and I are a different story. I used to call them, and they would be pleasant on the phone. However, the phone never rang the other way from them. After a while, I felt if they cared about me, they would call me once in a while, but they don't. I have chosen to love them from a distance. The only time I do hear from them is if someone dies. Amazing? You can choose to waste a lot of time trying to figure out the why, but in the end, you are wasting time in your life when you could be working on helping yourself and others by being the person you were meant to be. Sure it's upsetting, and some would say you need to be close to your family, but if your family is not there for you, there truly is no point.

Chapter 15

Importance of Having A Plan "B"

When I was in high school, I didn't really apply myself as I should have. Although, I did pass all of my classes. I never liked the whole school atmosphere. I felt it was very competitive and judgmental instead of a place to excel at your own pace. There was always someone smarter, better, athletically inclined, and then there were the teachers. At least the teachers I had focused more on the students who excelled in their class and more or less ignored the rest of us.

What I didn't think about were the consequences of that type of thinking. I didn't care about college after graduation. I chose to get married and have someone who would take care of me for the rest of my life. And life would just fall into place, marriage, kids, house, no more worries. WRONG! If I had had a plan "B," I never would have fallen into that situation or at least not to such extremes.

I had no plan "B," so when my marriage didn't work out, I had to work my way from the ground up. I could have saved myself a lot of grief if I had had a plan "B" in place back then. If I had money stashed away, I could have taken care of most everything after my divorce, including taking care of my son.

No one should ever feel stuck in a job they have, even if they have been at that job for a long time. Everyone should have a plan "B" for their career. If life is not working out as you had planned, and you have no plan "B" to fall back on, these are some of the effects it could have on you at work.

#1 You are probably negative to others and don't even realize it.

#2 You're not helping yourself or the company you work for by going to work unhappy.

#3 You don't care, so you are not going to give it your all.

I have had a few jobs in different places. One thing I have learned that they all have in common is that you don't have to be the sharpest tool in the shed to get what you want. It comes down to creativity.

I have worked in accounting for many years now. I did take some accounting classes in college, but I have no degree. In changing jobs, although I still do not have a degree, the experiences I have taken away from each employer made me more valuable as an employee. I have had better chances at landing other jobs because of this previous work experience.

I am sixty-four as I am sitting here writing this novel. It absolutely drives me crazy when someone thinks they are too old for a job that no one would hire them or me at this age. I beg to differ. With that attitude, you are setting yourself up for failure before you've even tried. I've never written a novel before, but here I am at least trying.

Just recently, I decided to change jobs. In my case, it was not the job or the people I was unhappy with, but other companies in my area were offering more benefits. When you're older like I am, the benefits are important and necessary.

I applied for a job at a company not far from where I live. A week and a half later, they called me in for an interview. Before an interview, I get all my ducks in a row. I notate what I am looking for and what work atmosphere suits me best. I know that I need to work where I am part of a team, not segregated, and I always notate what I do best. If you really want a job you have to sell yourself. Don't let them do all the talking and walk away without asking questions. I think interviewers like it when you ask questions. I also had a letter of recommendation from a previous employer who stated they would definitely hire me back. I never show the letter unless I am interested in the job, otherwise, there is no point in using it. I felt the interview went well. They told me they had more people to interview and would get back to me. That is something I have heard many times before.

The following day, they called and told me when they wanted me to start, offering me the same pay with many new benefits. I accepted the job and was happy about it, but now I had to sit down and discuss this with my current employer. I spoke with the president of the company. He offered to pay me more but couldn't compete with the benefits the other job was offering. He told me to sleep on it and let him know the next day. I told him the following day I was going to take the new job. He stated he understood but said if I ended up not liking it to please come back. He let me know that there would always be work there for me. I really appreciated his kindness. That is my plan "B". Now, no matter what happens, I will still have a job either way.

Playing it safe in life leaves you with missed opportunities. One should take chances and risks sometimes in life. You have to think outside the box and do what works best for your well-being. Only you know exactly what is best for you.

It is so important to have a game plan for your life. When you don't have a plan, you can feel stuck. I felt stuck many times in life, in marriages, living situations, and jobs. I never took the time to re-evaluate what wasn't working and instead chose to blame others and be miserable.

Take the plunge. Do something you've been putting off or fix something that now needs your attention. Make a bucket list and start doing the things on that list, no matter how old or young you are.

If you always do what you always did, you'll always get what you always got.

Every single person on this earth goes through problems in life. No one in life is left out. You can choose to be angry, feel sorry for yourself, blame others, or you can take the time and look at situations differently. Why did this happen? How can I resolve it? How can I be happy again? What can I do to change it?

Time is a gift. It seems as though when life gets so busy with everything, we don't stop to take time to just sit down in a quiet place to realize what is going on. As crazy as this sounds, I get up an hour and a half early every morning before work so I can sit and plan my day. If I just got up and got ready and left, I would be miserable.

No one is promised tomorrow. Make your mark on life! Leave this world a better place than how you found it. You are of great value no matter what has happened in your life.

Somewhere in your day, you have to set aside some time for downtime, where you can look at your situation and evaluate what works for you.

We all deserve to be happy. Create the harmony you so desire in your life. The ball is in your court.

Acknowledgements:

I would like to thank all the doctors who helped me through my breast cancer. I am still here because of your skills and talents.

The American Cancer Society for providing the much-needed information to make a decision based on the most current data.

My son and his family, for always being there for me.

Patricia Carpenter for editing the book and encouraging me along the way. I couldn't have done this without you.

My parents, siblings, friends and last but not least my favorite pit bull, Drummer, in heaven, until we meet again.

About the Author

The author was born in Schenectady, NY, and attended Schoharie School. She now resides and works in Bradenton, Florida. She never owned another sailboat but would love to go out sailing again, one day.

You can follow her on Facebook, Community Book Chat for comments, reviews.

Email, briggsmindy3@gmail.com

References:

National Suicide Prevention 1-800-273-8255

www.suicidepreventionlifeline.org

Suicide & Depression 24/7 Free & Confidential

American Cancer Society 1-800-227-2345

www.cancer.org

Grief and Loss:

www.considerable.com

Hospice Foundation:

www.Hospicefoundation.org

Moving to a New City Alone:

www.travelsofadam.com

www.mymovingreviews.com

www.pods.com